# RIGHTING CANADA'S WRONGS

## Anti-Semitism and the MS *St. Louis*

### Canada's Anti-Semitic Immigration Policies in the Twentieth Century

Rona Arato

JAMES LORIMER & COMPANY LTD., PUBLISHERS
TORONTO

James Lorimer & Company Ltd., Publishers acknowledges funding support from the Ontario Arts Council (OAC), an agency of the Government of Ontario. We acknowledge the support of the Canada Council for the Arts, which last year invested $153 million to bring the arts to Canadians throughout the country. This project has been made possible in part by the Government of Canada and with the support of Ontario Creates.

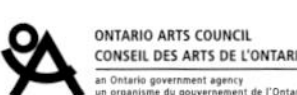

Cover design: Gwen North

Library and Archives Canada Cataloguing in Publication

Title: Anti-Semitism and the MS St. Louis : Canada's anti-Semitic immigration policies in the twentieth century / Rona Arato.
Names: Arato, Rona, author.
Series: Righting Canada's wrongs.
Description: Series statement: Righting Canada's wrongs | Includes bibliographical references and index.
Identifiers: Canadiana 20200213709 | ISBN 9781459415669 (hardcover)
Subjects: LCSH: St. Louis (Ship)—Juvenile literature. | LCSH: Anti-semitism—Canada—History—20th century—Juvenile literature. | LCSH: Canada—Emigration and immigration—Government policy—History—20th century—Juvenile literature. | LCSH: Jewish refugees—History—20th century—Juvenile literature. | LCSH: Jewish refugees—Government policy—Canada—History—20th century Juvenile literature. | LCSH: Holocaust, Jewish (1939–1945)—Juvenile literature. | LCSH: Jews—Canada—History—20th century—Juvenile literature. | LCSH: Jews—Germany—History—20th century—Juvenile literature.
Classification: LCC DS146.C2 A73 2020 | DDC j305.892/407109044—dc23

James Lorimer & Company Ltd., Publishers
117 Peter St., Suite 304
Toronto, ON, Canada
M5V 0M3
www.lorimer.ca

Printed and bound in South Korea
Manufactured by Prinpia Co., Ltd.
Job #FP2020-01

*For Cy, Samantha, Tali and Simon,*
*the next generation*

# Acknowledgements

Writing this book has been a rewarding experience. I am indebted to the people who helped me make the history come alive. Thank you to Peter and Gilda Spitz, who provided the story and photos of Peter's mother, Ursula, who was a child on the *St. Louis*. I had interviewed Ursula for the "Survivors of the Shoah Visual History" project, so it was especially gratifying to reconnect with her family.

Thank you to Ana Maria Gordon, who is the only *St. Louis* survivor living in Canada. I spent a delightful afternoon with Ana Maria as she shared her memories of the voyage. Her son Donald Gruner sent the photos that we have used in the book.

The "Tailor Project" that brought in hundreds of Jewish Holocaust survivors was, until recently, a relatively unknown story. I want to thank my friend Anne Dublin for her detailed account of how her family came to Canada through that program.

My editor, Pam Hickman, has been an invaluable partner in writing this book. Carrie Gleason, the publisher, has been a great help guiding me on what to include in the narrative.

And lastly, I would like to thank Prime Minister Justin Trudeau and the Canadian government for recognizing a wrong; apologizing on behalf of the Canadian people and vowing that this form of discrimination will never happen in Canada again.

# Contents



**WATCH THE VIDEO**

Look for this symbol throughout the book for links to video and audio clips available online.

Visit www.lorimer.ca/wrongs to see the entire series.

# Introduction

Jewish immigration to Canada began in the middle of the eighteenth century. The earliest Jews came as fur trappers, adventurers or members of the British army. Later waves of immigration were mostly from Eastern Europe and the Russian Empire where anti-Semitism (anti-Jewish racism), poverty and violent, government-sponsored persecution propelled Jews to search for a better life. From 1881 to 1914, two million Jews left Eastern Europe, most immigrating to the United States and many to Canada. At the time, Canada was looking for immigrants to populate its vast country. Farmers, labourers and skilled workers were all in high demand.

During the 1920s and 30s, immigrants to Canada were viewed as unwanted competition for already scarce jobs. There was a significant increase in anti-immigration sentiment and, especially, anti-Jewish protests. The rise of Hitler and Nazism in Germany fueled these attitudes. As conditions for Jews in Germany worsened, Canada closed its doors to Jewish immigrants. At a time when Jews were desperate to escape from Nazi Germany, widespread anti-Semitism was a major factor in keeping them out of Canada. In 1939, Canada's head of immigration, Frederick Blair, was asked how many Jews Canada should accept. He replied, "None is too many."

This attitude culminated in "The *St. Louis* Affair." In 1939, Canadian Prime Minister Mackenzie King refused to allow a ship of over 900 Jewish refugees, who were fleeing Nazi Germany, to enter the country. In this book, you will read about some of the families who were on board and what became of them. You will meet Ana Maria Karman who was four years old when she sailed on the ship with her family. She is the last Canadian survivor of the voyage and was interviewed for this book. Teens Eric and Ursula Spitz were also on the ship Canada turned away. The ship was forced to return to Europe where many of the passengers died during the war.

During the Second World War, thousands of Canadian Jews served in the armed forces. At the same time, organizations such as the Canadian Jewish Congress fought a losing battle with the Canadian government to accept more Jewish refugees. After the war, a booming economy and labour shortages encouraged the government to open Canada's doors to increased immigration. Jewish refugees, most of whom were Holocaust survivors, came to restart lives destroyed during the war. Among them were over a thousand Jewish boys and girls who came as part of the War Orphans Project. Another project, the Tailor Project, brought in 2,200 skilled tailors, half of whom were Jewish Holocaust survivors.

In the 1950s and 60s, attitudes toward Jews and other minorities began to change. In the 1970s, Prime Minister Pierre Elliott Trudeau encouraged the concept of multiculturalism and acceptance of people from all over the world. Jewish immigrants who came during this period achieved success in many fields, including business, science, medicine and arts.

Today, Canada strives to celebrate its multicultural society. Part of this policy involves recognizing past wrongs and apologizing on behalf of previous governments. In 2018, Prime Minister Justin Trudeau issued a formal apology to survivors of the *St. Louis* for Canada's role in the tragedy, as well as to all Jewish Canadians for the discrimination that they and their families have experienced in Canada.

PROLOGUE

# THE RESILIENCE OF JEWISH CULTURE THROUGH HISTORY

Jews are an ethnic and religious group of people who originated in the Middle East over 5,000 years ago and follow a religion called Judaism. It is commonly believed that Jews were slaves in Egypt about 3,000 years ago. According to their belief, God freed them and gave Moses the Torah which sets out laws that Jews follow. After the Jews left Egypt, God promised them their own land they called Israel. They made Jerusalem their capital and built the Temple, which was a centre for worship. Around 600 BCE, Babylonia (present-day Iraq) invaded the Kingdom of Judah (present-day Israel), destroyed Jerusalem and burned the Temple. The Jews were deported to Babylonia. The exile lasted for 70 years until the Jews were allowed to return to their land. They rebuilt Jerusalem and the Temple. About 2,000 years ago, Rome conquered what was then called Judea. After a series of revolts, the Romans destroyed Jerusalem and the Second Temple, and deported the Jews. Many fled to Babylonia, Northern Africa, Spain and Portugal. Others were taken to Rome as slaves or labourers. This began what is known as the Diaspora (Jews living outside Israel). Jews who went to Spain and Portugal are called Sephardic, after the Hebrew word *Sepharad* for Spain. Jews who went to Western and Eastern Europe are called Ashkenazi, from the Hebrew word for German. Jews now live around the world but throughout history have been the victims of anti-Jewish beliefs and behaviours.

**History of anti-Semitism**

The term "anti-Semitism" refers to prejudice or discrimination against Jews as individuals and as a group. Jews have been persecuted throughout history. In Ancient Greece and Rome, Jews were persecuted for their determination to practice their religion rather than adopting the social and religious customs of the society. After Christianity spread throughout Europe, Jews were often forced to live in separate neighbourhoods called ghettos, and to wear a yellow badge or other symbol to identify themselves as Jews. They were not granted citizenship in most European countries until the late 1700s and early 1800s. In the late 1800s and early 1900s, Jews in Russia and other European countries faced violent anti-Jewish riots called pogroms. Thousands of Jews were killed. Millions of Jews fled Europe for Canada and other countries.

**Synagogues**

Jewish houses of worship are called synagogues, pictured on the left. Spiritual leaders are called rabbis, which means "teachers." Most synagogues also have a cantor, who chants the service. Synagogues serve as the centre of Jewish life. They provide a sanctuary for services and are used for study, social gatherings and community events. Synagogues have been used by Jewish people since the Babylonian exile.

**Celebrating children**

Life events are celebrated in special ways. In a brit milah, a Jewish boy is circumcised and named eight days after his birth. Jewish girls are named in a baby naming ceremony. Bar and bat mitzvah mean "son and daughter of the commandment." Each is a coming of age ceremony that boys celebrate at thirteen and girls at twelve or thirteen years old. To prepare, they study Jewish history and customs with a rabbi and cantor, and learn to read Hebrew so they can chant a portion of the Torah in front of a congregation.

**The Torah**

The Torah, pictured here, is the first five books of the Hebrew Bible, including the Ten Commandments. Shabbat, which involves refraining from work activities and engaging in rest, is the only ritual observance written in the Ten Commandments. It is observed from sunset on Friday to sunset on Saturday as a day of rest and spiritual enrichment.

**Menorah**

Judaism's most ancient symbol is the menorah, the official symbol of Israel. The Hanukkah menorah, left, holds nine candles — one for each night of Hanukkah plus an extra candle, called the Shamash, used to light all of the others. The feast of Hanukkah commemorates Jewish victory in 167 BCE over the Greeks. The six-pointed Star of David in the centre is a common symbol of Judaism.

**Welcome to a Jewish home**

A Mezuzah, pictured here, is a case attached to a doorpost to signify a Jewish home. The case contains a handwritten parchment scroll from the Torah stating: "The words that I shall tell you this day: that you shall love your God, believe only in Him, keep His commandments, and pass all of this on to your children."

**What is kosher food?**

Observant Jewish people only eat food identified as kosher. They only eat cloven-hooved animals, such as sheep, cattle and goats, that chew their cud. Kosher law permits only fish with fins and scales. Shellfish are not kosher. Meat and dairy cannot be eaten together. Only certain birds, including chicken, ducks and geese, are kosher.

**Special holidays**

Jews have several special celebrations throughout the year, based on the Jewish calendar. Rosh Hashanah, the Jewish New Year, is in the fall. Yom Kippur, a day of fasting and reflection, comes ten days later. Hanukkah is celebrated for eight days in December, and Passover, which commemorates the Jewish exodus from Egypt, is always in the spring. During Passover, Jews eat matzo, pictured here, to symbolize the unleavened bread that they took with them when fleeing Egypt.

CHAPTER 1
# COME TO CANADA

## Leaving Europe

Early Jewish immigrants to Canada in the 1700s and early 1800s were mainly European adventurers, explorers and entrepreneurs. In the mid to late 1800s, life in Europe became very difficult and dangerous due to growing anti-Semitism (hostility against Jews), pogroms (organized massacres of an ethnic group) and economic hardship. More Jews decided to leave. This second wave of Jewish immigrants was mostly peasants, farmers and labourers.

**Where Jewish immigrants came from**
Many Jewish immigrants came to Canada in the late 1800s and early 1900s from countries in eastern Europe.

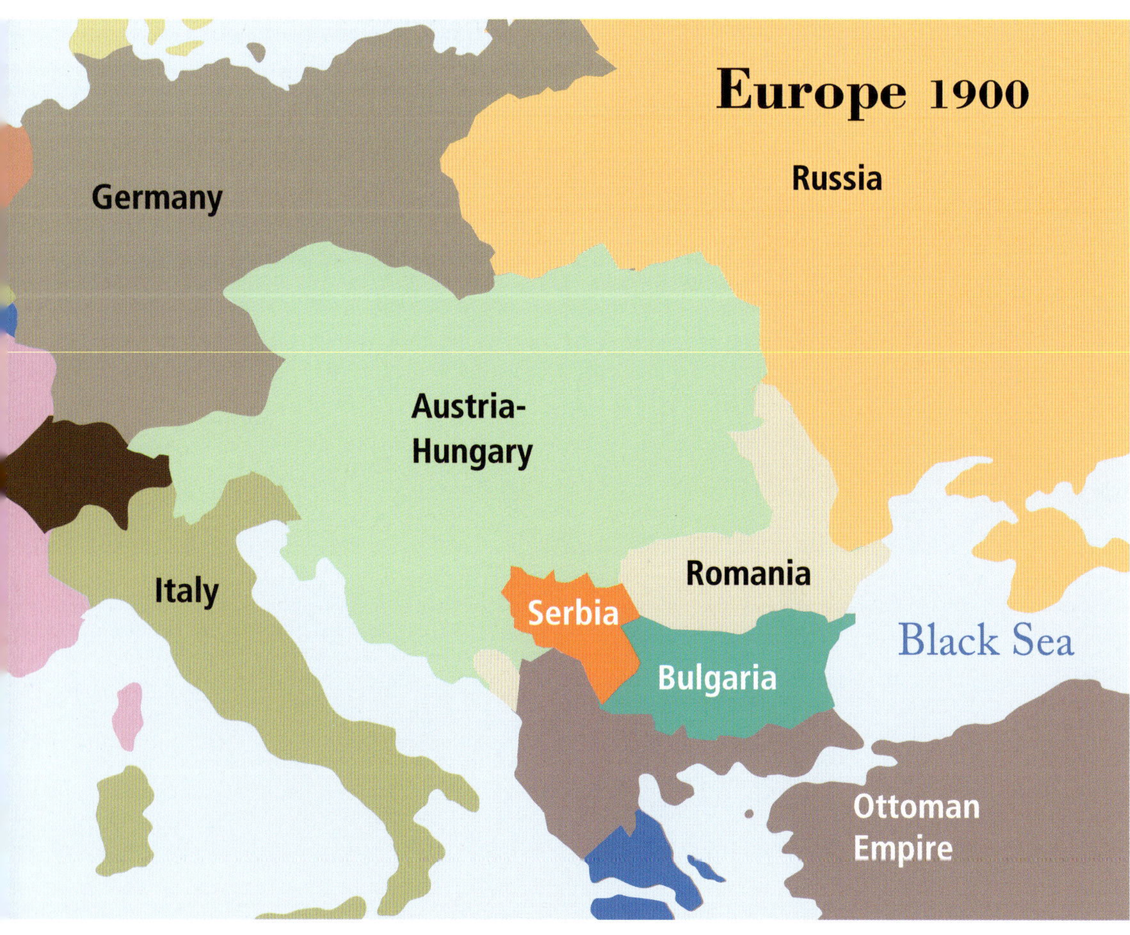

**Poland's Jews**
Since 1264, Jews have lived in Krakow, Poland, pictured above, in what was known as Austria-Hungary until 1918. Life became very difficult in the late 1800s due to rising anti-Semitism and violence against Jews. Many decided to leave their country and seek a safer and better life in Canada.

**Europe's largest synagogue in Hungary**
The Dohány Street Synagogue, pictured here, was built in Budapest, Hungary in the 1850s. Many Hungarian Jews came to Canada in the late 1800s and early 1900s to escape mounting persecution. Jewish immigrants built new synagogues in Canada to replace those they left behind.

**Resisting oppression in Lithuania**
Jews in Czarist Russia fought against oppression, but conditions didn't improve. Above, people gather for a funeral for revolutionaries who fought for better living conditions, and basic human rights in Vilna, Lithuania, a part of the Russian Empire in 1905.

## Life in Europe became very difficult and dangerous for Jews in the 1930s.

**Ukrainian war orphans**
The Ukrainian War of Independence left thousands of children without parents, homes or means of survival. Their only hope was to leave and find new homes in other countries. These Ukrainian Jewish war orphans are pictured in 1921 in Rovno, Ukraine, formerly part of the Russian Empire, before leaving for Canada.

Thousands of children were without parents, homes or means of survival.

**They came from Russia**

Anti-Jewish violence in Russia led many Jewish families like this one to leave their homes and businesses in Russia and start over. This family is pictured in their own restaurant in Kishinev, Russia (now Moldova), in 1923, shortly before they emigrated.

**Ship of dreams**

These immigrants are on their way to Canada where a new life full of possibilities awaits.

# A new life of possibilities awaits.

# Settling in Canada

Jewish immigrants settled across Canada, from coast to coast. While some Jews became attracted to the gold rush on the West Coast, and some settled in farm communities in Manitoba and Saskatchewan, most preferred to live in urban areas. Nova Scotia and New Brunswick also attracted Jewish immigrants. Wherever Jews settled, they built synagogues and started Jewish schools and organizations. Jews, like other immigrant communities, tended to live together. By the outbreak of the First World War in 1914, there were approximately 100,000 Canadian Jews, of whom three-quarters lived in either Montreal or Toronto. Jews had established themselves in every major Canadian city and in many small towns.

**Entrepreneurs**
A group of about one hundred Jews came to Victoria, British Columbia, in 1858. They opened shops to supply prospectors arriving from China and the Far East on their way north to the Cariboo Gold Rush. The small Jewish community built a synagogue in Victoria in 1862. Simon Leiser, pictured left, was a Jewish immigrant from Germany who joined the community in 1880. He ran several successful businesses in Victoria, including this wholesale grocery chain, pictured below.

**Baron Maurice de Hirsch**
Baron de Hirsch, pictured above, was a wealthy European Jewish financier who funded charities around the world to help Jewish immigrants settle in new countries. He was instrumental in bringing Jewish immigrants to settle and farm the Canadian prairies.

## Jewish immigrants settled across Canada, from coast to coast.

## JEWISH FARM COLONIES and SETTLEMENTS on the PRAIRIES

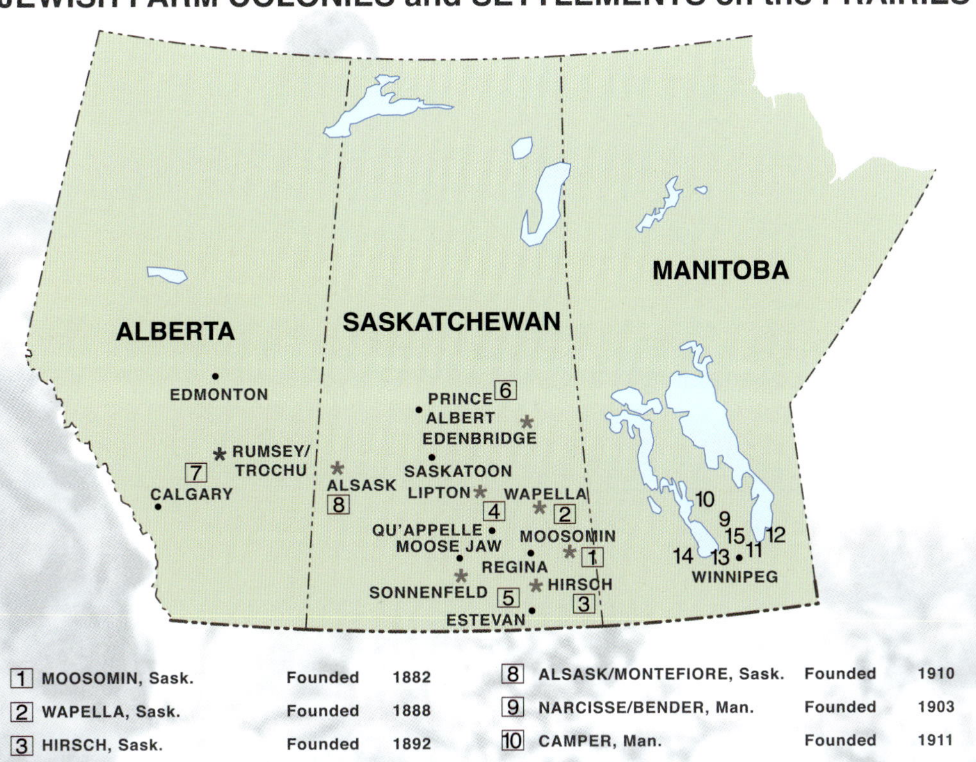


| | | | |
|---|---|---|---|
| 1 | MOOSOMIN, Sask. | Founded | 1882 |
| 2 | WAPELLA, Sask. | Founded | 1888 |
| 3 | HIRSCH, Sask. | Founded | 1892 |
| 4 | LIPTON, Sask. | Founded | 1901 |
| 5 | SONNENFELD, Sask. | Founded | 1906 |
| 6 | EDENBRIDGE, Sask. | Founded | 1906 |
| 7 | RUMSEY/TROCHU, Alta. | Founded | 1906 |
| 8 | ALSASK/MONTEFIORE, Sask. | Founded | 1910 |
| 9 | NARCISSE/BENDER, Man. | Founded | 1903 |
| 10 | CAMPER, Man. | Founded | 1911 |

11 BIRDS HILL
12 PINE RIDGE
13 WEST ILDONAN
14 ROSENFELD
15 ROSSER

} Manitoba farm settlements founded during and after the First World War.

* FARM COLONY • PRINCIPAL CITY

**Winnipeg Jewish neighbourhood**
Winnipeg became home to a large Jewish population. This image shows the Jewish neighbourhood, also called the Jewish Quarter, in 1904.

**Settling the Prairies**
In the late 1800s, the Canadian government wanted to settle the west and urged immigrants to farm the land there. This map of the prairies (above) shows Jewish farm colonies and settlements between 1882 and the 1920s.

**New Hirsch colony, Manitoba**
The new Hirsch colony, pictured here in 1910, was funded by the Jewish Colonization Association of London. It was named after Baron de Hirsch who helped many Jewish immigrants settle on the prairies.

**Saskatchewan, 1916**
These Jewish children are thriving in the fresh air and healthy environment of Saskatchewan.

**Settling in Montreal**
Montreal's Shaar Hashomayim Synagogue is pictured here on Kensington Avenue in the early 1900s.

**New kind of fun**
Their new country opened up new experiences. These Jewish boys are posing with their baseball team at Fletcher's Field in Montreal, 1905.

## Most Jewish immigrants preferred to settle in cities.

**Newsboys**
These young Jewish boys earned money in 1910 by selling newspapers on the streets of Toronto.

**Unfair wages**
These Jewish workers are pictured in a Toronto textile factory in 1907. Women often earned less than one dollar for an eighty-hour week. Children worked for no pay as "learners."

NUMBER 4084

SHARES One

The Toronto Labor Lyceum Association, Limited

This Certifies that Mr. F. Wallerstein is the owner of One Shares of the Capital Stock of The Toronto Labor Lyceum Association, Limited transferable only on the books of this Corporation in person or by Attorney upon surrender of this Certificate properly endorsed.

In Witness Whereof the said Corporation has caused this Certificate to be signed by its duly authorized officers and its Corporate Seal to be hereunto affixed this day of Nov. A.D. 1925

Secretary

President

SHARES $5.00 EACH

**Labour unions**
Jewish labour unions fought for better working conditions and pay for their workers. When workers joined the union, they could share in the benefits. This certificate shows membership in the Labour Lyceum, a centre of Jewish union activity on Spadina Avenue, Toronto.

**Cramped quarters in Toronto's Ward District**
Many Jews came to Canada to raise their children in a safe and free society. Most Jewish immigrants preferred to settle in cities, such as Toronto. This home is in the Toronto neighbourhood centred on Bay and Albert Streets known as "the Ward," where many Jews and other immigrants lived. Often two families would share a home to save money.

WATCH THE VIDEO

**A Canadian education**
Learning English was key to becoming Jewish Canadians. Children of Jewish immigrants are seen here learning alongside others at Brant Street Public School in Toronto.

**The fight for a Jewish homeland**
Toronto's Jewish community was politically active early on. Romanian Jewish immigrant women are seen here in 1920, rallying in support of a Jewish homeland in Palestine.

Watch the video at
http://bit.ly/rcwstlouis01

**Mount Sinai Hospital**
Jewish doctors were not allowed to practice in most Canadian hospitals so the community founded Mount Sinai Hospital on Yorkville Avenue, Toronto, in 1924. Pictured here in the 1920s are members of the Mount Sinai Hospital Ladies' Auxiliary with Dorothy Dworkin, pictured at the centre. She was a Jewish Canadian nurse, businesswoman and philanthropist.

**First Jews settle in New Brunswick**
Beginning in the 1850s, a small group of Jewish immigrants settled in Saint John, New Brunswick. The first to arrive were Solomon Hart, pictured here, and his wife Alice, from England. The first synagogue, Ahavath Achim (Brotherly Love), was dedicated in 1899 and served about thirty families.

**Green's cigar store**
Some early Jewish immigrants to Saint John became affluent cigar makers. This image shows Nathan Green, right, outside his store which sold expensive cigars from Havana, Cuba. A second wave of Jewish immigrants arrived between 1892 and the 1920s. Many men were peddlers who ended up opening stores and factories along Main, Mill and Dock Streets in Saint John, New Brunswick.

**Glace Bay, Cape Breton, Nova Scotia**
Jewish immigrants came to Glace Bay, Cape Breton, pictured here, for work. They were recruited by the Glace Bay Coal Company to work as labourers and miners.

## Jewish doctors were not allowed to practice in most Canadian hospitals.

# Early Canadian Society

Canadian society was heavily influenced by its former French and British colonial powers. Even after Canada became a country in 1867, it remained part of the British Empire. Outside of Quebec, English-speaking Canadians were mainly British Protestants; Quebec's citizens were primarily French-speaking Roman Catholics. Other cultures, including First Nations, were treated as inferior, or worse. Anti-Jewish sentiments existed in Canadian society from the country's earliest days. Although Jews made up only 1 per cent of the population in Quebec, they were denounced in newspapers and barred from sitting on school boards and holding government positions and other jobs. In English Canada, Jews were excluded from many professions. There were no Jewish judges and few Jewish teachers in public schools. Many industries did not hire Jews. Professional schools and universities had Jewish quotas, or limits, to the number of Jewish students they would accept. Jewish professionals such as lawyers, engineers and nurses often hid their identity to succeed. Some changed their names to find work in their fields since some names were easily identified as Jewish. For example, Shapiro might be changed to Sharpe. Canadian Jews faced racism in their daily lives yet they persevered and helped Canada grow and prosper.

**British influences**
Even after Confederation in 1867, Canada was greatly influenced by the British Empire. The Union Jack, pictured here, was Canada's flag, the same as Britain's. Canada did not get its own flag, the Maple Leaf, until 1965.

"ANGLO-SAXON TORONTO"

**The persecuted**
Minorities suffered discrimination in both English- and French-speaking Canada. In this 1906 Quebec cartoon, a Jew (left) and an Asian man (right) share their feelings of persecution. Each is illustrated in an unflattering way. The Jew appears to be a peddler while the Asian man is carrying a load of laundry, both racist stereotypes. Baptiste, in the centre, represents French Canada who is trying to drive the other two away.

CES PAUVRES PERSÉCUTÉS

**Multicultural**
Immigrants from many countries settled in Toronto and Montreal. This cartoon tries to reflect the multicultural nature of Toronto in the early 1900s, despite being called "the most thoroughly Anglo-Saxon city in North America." A Jewish man is pictured far left.

**Canada joins Britain in the First World War**
The First World War (1914–18) began when Germany invaded France through Belgium. When Great Britain declared war on Germany, Canada and other members of the British Empire followed. This recruiting poster encourages Canadian men to enlist and fight against Germany with the Allied forces (initially the British Empire, France and Russia).

**Reputation for bravery**
During the war, Canadian soldiers exhibited great fighting skills and exceptional bravery. They are seen here in the trenches in France where much of the war was fought. Canada gained international respect for its leadership and contributions to the Allied forces. Its new reputation strengthened its political independence from Britain and distinguished it as more than just a part of the British Empire.

## Anti-Jewish sentiments existed in Canada from its earliest days.

**Canada matures as a nation**
During the Paris Peace Conference in June 1919, the Treaty of Versailles was signed (pictured here). Due to Canada's valiant fighting with the Allied forces, it earned a seat at the table. By participating in the Conference, Canada took charge of its own foreign policy. The Treaty set out the terms of surrender for Germany, who started the war and lost. Harsh penalties were imposed on Germany. German citizens suffered through the next two decades, building up resentment and anger against the British Empire and its allies.

CHAPTER 2

# ANTI-SEMITISM IN GERMANY

## The Rise of Hitler

The First World War ended on November 11, 1918, when Germany surrendered. The Treaty of Versailles forced Germany to surrender land and demanded stiff reparation payments. To ensure that Germany would never again start a war, it was prohibited from rearming. The terms of the treaty led to great hardship and humiliation for the German people. This resulted in a growing sense of resentment and unrest during the years between the two World Wars. The German economy suffered from the staggering amount of reparations and the devastation caused by the war (over 1.7 million German soldiers had died; 12,000 of them Jewish). High inflation, that is soaring prices, made money almost worthless.

Watch the video at http://bit.ly/rcwstlouis50

Adolph Hitler understood that Germans needed someone to blame for their troubles. And that someone, he decided, would be the Jews. Hitler was the leader of the National Socialist German Workers' Party, also known as the Nazi Party. It supported a form of government called National Socialism, a type of fascism. The Nazi Party believed in strong nationalism, military power, a single dictator and hatred of communism, along with a virulent dose of anti-Semitism. As conditions worsened, many young people became attracted to his ideas. They blamed the Jews for Germany's economic troubles and vowed to restore the country to its prewar greatness.

**Adolf Hitler**
Adolf Hitler was born in Austria in 1889 and moved to Germany in 1913, at the age of 24. He served in the German Army during the First World War. In 1919, Hitler joined the German Workers' Party which became the National Socialist German Worker's Party, or Nazi Party, in 1920. Hitler took over as the party's leader in 1921.

**The swastika**
The swastika pictured here was the symbol for the Nazi Party.

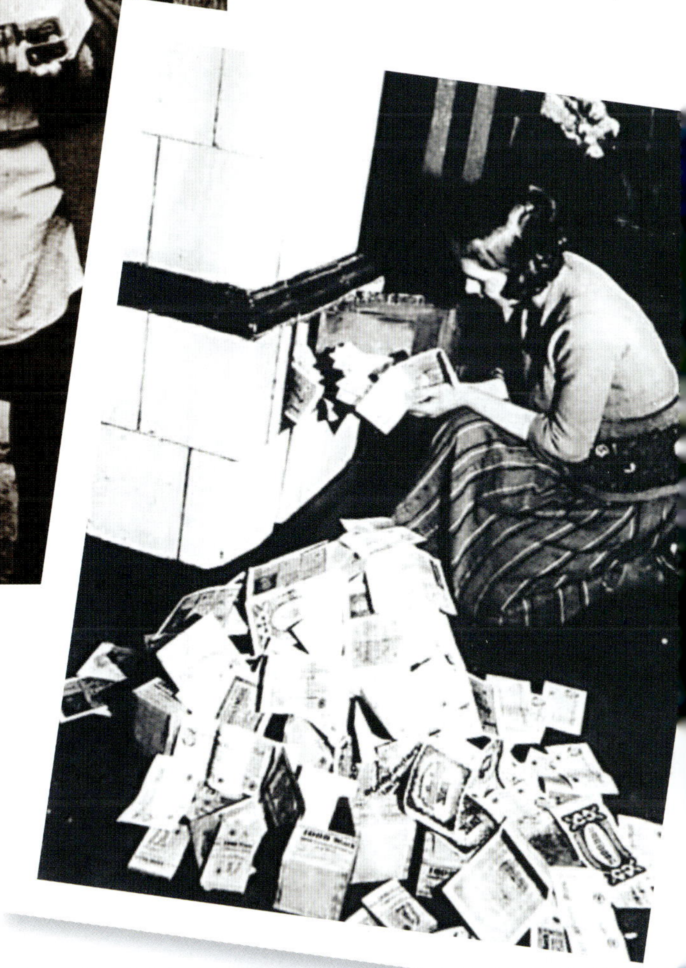

**Worthless money**
Following the First World War and the Treaty of Versailles, Germany's economy collapsed. Inflation was out of control, and German money became virtually worthless. Above, a child plays with stacks of money, using them as building bricks. To the right, a woman lights her fire with paper money.

## Hyperinflation in Germany between the wars

### Price of a loaf of bread in Germany

(the equivalent of US dollars at the time)

1914: $0.13
1919: $0.26
1920: $700.00
Mar. 1923: $1,200.00
Sept. 1923: $2 million
Oct. 1923: $670 million
Nov. 1923: $3 billion
Dec. 1923: $100 billion

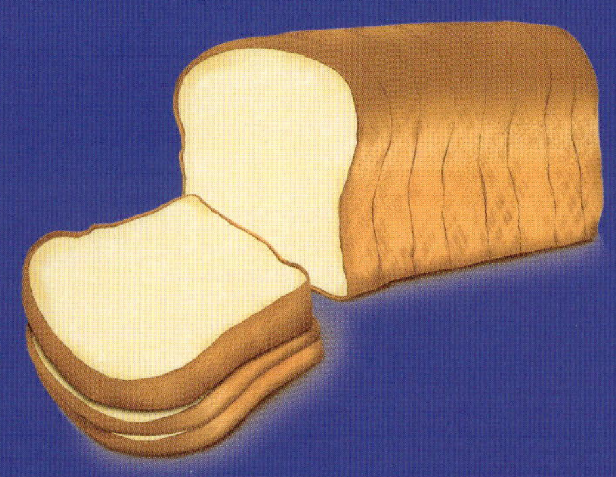

**Mein Kampf (My Struggle)**
Adolf Hitler wrote this book in the 1920s while in prison for trying to overthrow the German government. He stated that Jews and communists were evil and should be destroyed. He also outlined his vision for the Third Reich, a renewed Germany built on a pure, master race. He wrote,"… men do not perish by the loss of wars, but by the loss … of pure blood." His five year sentence was reduced to nine months, and he and his Nazi party quickly gained political power. Hitler became chancellor of Germany and fuehrer (leader) of the German people in 1933.

**Anti-Jewish exhibition**
This exhibition was part of the Nazis' anti-Semitic propaganda campaign. Called *The Eternal Jew*, the posters claimed to show "typical external features" of Jews so that citizens could identify their Jewish neighbours and later turn them in to authorities.

**Anti-Semitic propaganda**
In this image, a German Nazi tacks up an anti-Jewish poster that reads: "Germans defend yourselves against Jewish atrocities and propaganda." Life became increasingly difficult and dangerous for German Jews due to the widespread Nazi propaganda.

**Hitler quote**
This poster is a quote by Adolf Hitler. Its translation reads, "Should the international Jewish financiers succeed once again in plunging the nations into a world war, the result will be not the victory of Jews but the annihilation of the Jewish race in Europe." Hitler was preparing the German people for war and blaming the Jews for it.

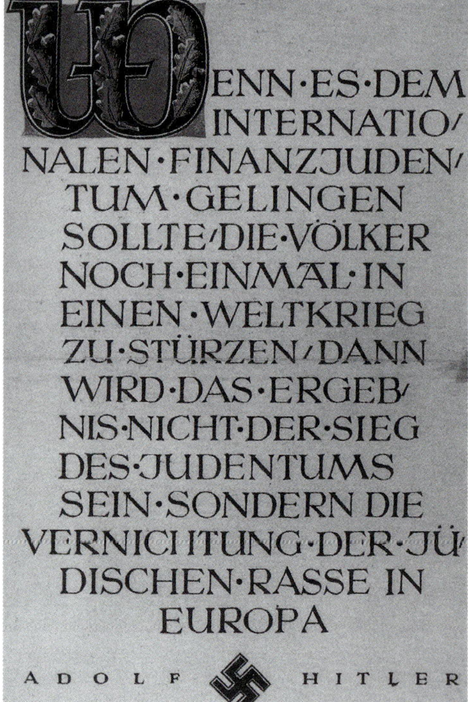

**Concentration camps**

In the 1930s, the Nazis began setting up prison camps called concentration camps. They rounded up leaders of political, social and cultural groups who the Nazis thought could cause trouble for them. Any leader who was opposed to Hitler's new government was imprisoned in a concentration camp without a charge or a trial. It was a way of scaring people into silence. The first Nazi concentration camp was Dachau, pictured here, established near Munich in March 1933. Later on, the concentration camps became filled with all the groups the Nazis targetted, including Jews, the Romani (then called Gypsies, a slur), Poles and people from other Slavic countries, along with people who had physical or mental disabilities. Homosexuals, Black people and Jehovah's Witnesses were also considered inferior and undesirable in Germany.

## Any leader who opposed Hitler was imprisoned in a concentration camp.

**The Nuremberg Laws**

In 1935, Hitler's Nazi Party passed several new laws that became known as the Nuremberg Laws. One of the first things they did was take away Jewish Germans' citizenship and voting rights. This effectively made it legal to persecute Jews. Jews lost all of their basic rights and could not protest their harsh treatment. The Nuremberg Laws also banned marriage and sexual relations between Jews and non-Jews, calling it "race pollution" that was punishable by imprisonment. Hitler believed that certain members of the German race, called Aryans, were superior to all others. Two of the main features of Aryans were their blue eyes and blond hair. He planned breeding programs of German Aryans to secure a future that would make all Germans of this "superior" race. This fueled public hatred against other races, especially Jews. This poster warns against interracial relationships and attempts to justify and explain the Nuremberg Laws.

# Need to Escape

Hitler's Nazi government passed laws restricting the rights of Jews. Jewish children were kicked out of public schools, and Jewish teachers were dismissed. The Nazis created their own school books full of propaganda to convince German children to hate the Jews and other minorities. It was becoming painfully clear that German Jews were in grave danger. Jews, desperate to leave Germany, lined up for hours and even days at the Canadian, US and other embassies seeking visas. For most, the effort was futile. The US and Canada had passed legislation closing their doors to immigrants. Britain took thousands, but only a few other countries accepted any. They were trapped in Germany, with a government that wanted to destroy them.

THE TORONTO DAILY STAR

TORONTO, MONDAY, APRIL 24, 1933—36 PAGES

TWO CENTS

SHUT GERMAN SCHOOLS TO WEED OUT JEWS

ALL GERMAN SCHOOLS ON ENFORCED HOLIDAY "PURGING" IS PLANNED

MAY DEFER ACTION ON WATERWAY PACT

CITY DIRECTED TO PAY $25,000 FOR PARK SITE

HOME AND SPORT EDITION

PIERRE VAN PAASSEN IS NOT A JEW

KING GEORGE PLANNED TO BECOME DICTATOR IF COALITION FAILED

"INSIDE STORY" TOLD

FIND MONEY ORDERS ARE BEING "RAISED"

JEWS MUST BE EXTIRPATED BY ANY MEANS, SAYS HITLER

MISSIONARY RISKS DEATH TO DESTROY VOODOO MYTH

**Canadians kept informed**
Pierre van Paassen, a foreign correspondent for the *Toronto Star* newspaper, reported on atrocities committed against Jews by the Nazis after Hitler seized power in Germany.

**German Jewish businesses**
Many Jewish families owned businesses which catered to non-Jews as well. Here we see Jewish storekeepers in front of their gourmet food store in Berlin, Germany. It would soon be destroyed.

## Jewish children were kicked out of public schools.

**Kristallnacht**
On November 9–10, 1938, the Nazi party paramilitary group, called the SA, or Brown Shirts, ran through Germany and Austria smashing Jewish property, burning synagogues and attacking Jews. The violence became known as Kristallnacht (Night of Broken Glass) because of all the glass broken in Jewish homes and businesses like this one.

WATCH THE VIDEO

**Burning synagogues**
This synagogue is burning in Berlin after Nazi Brown Shirts set it on fire during Kristallnacht on November 9–10, 1938.

**Reaction to violence**
Passersby, some smiling, others looking bewildered, observe a demolished and looted Jewish shop in Berlin after Kristallnacht.

Watch the video at http://bit.ly/rcwstlouis02

**Jews expelled from Germany**
These Jews were forced to leave their homes in Germany and cross the border into Poland in 1938. As the danger for Jews escalated, they looked to other countries to take them in. Over 400,000 refugees fled Germany between 1933 and 1939. German and Austrian nationals who held American visas went to Britain. Many were released from Nazi concentration camps on the condition that they emigrate. America sponsored a number of Jewish intellectuals. Many countries, however, used the fear of a "fifth column" to close their doors to Jewish refugees. A "fifth column" means a dangerous group of immigrants who could act as spies or worse, once they were let in. Governments did not trust anyone from Germany, even Jews. Canada admitted the lowest number of Jewish refugees among developed nations.

## Where did German Jews go?

**Number of German Jewish refugees accepted, by country, between 1933 and 1945**

| | |
|---|---|
| United States: | 200,000 |
| Britain: | 70,000 |
| Palestine: | 125,000 |
| Canada: | 5,000 |

# Saving Children

By 1938, it became clear that Germany was no longer safe for Jews. Germany took over Austria and began to expand its empire throughout Europe. Jewish parents, frantic to save their children, put them on trains to get them away from the Nazis. In 1938–40, Great Britain took in 10,000 children from Nazi Germany, Nazi-occupied Austria, Czechoslovakia, Poland and the Free City of Danzig. Jewish organizations inside Germany and Britain planned the kindertransport, which in German means "children's transport." They chose children who were in imminent danger because their parents were in concentration camps or could no longer support them. The children traveled, unaccompanied by adults, by train to ports in Belgium and the Netherlands. From there they sailed to Harwich, England.

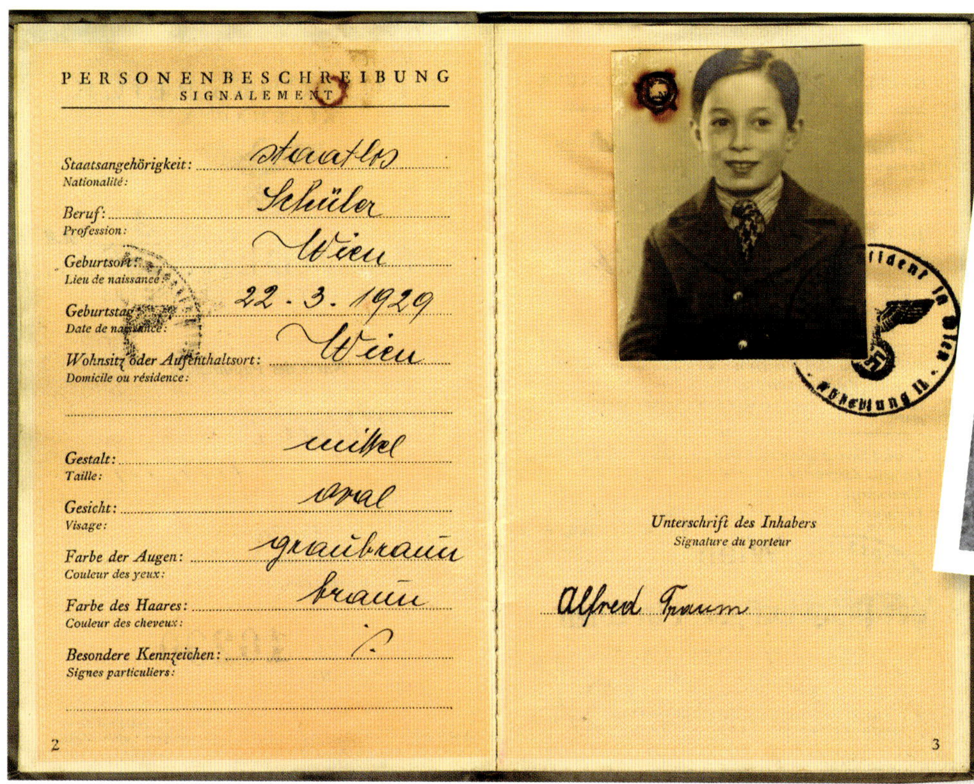

PERSONENBESCHREIBUNG
SIGNALEMENT

Staatsangehörigkeit: staatlos
Nationalité:
Beruf: Schüler
Profession:
Geburtsort: Wien
Lieu de naissance:
Geburtstag: 22. 3. 1929
Date de naissance:
Wohnsitz oder Aufenthaltsort: Wien
Domicile ou résidence:
Gestalt: mittel
Taille:
Gesicht: oval
Visage:
Farbe der Augen: graubraun
Couleur des yeux:
Farbe des Haares: braun
Couleur des cheveux:
Besondere Kennzeichen: ?
Signes particuliers:

2

Unterschrift des Inhabers
Signature du porteur
Alfred Traum

3

**Ready to go**
Ten-year-old Alfred Traum was issued this passport prior to his departure from Vienna, Austria, as part of the kindertransport.

**On their way**
Trains carrying Jewish refugee children stopped in Belgium where this photo was taken. From here, the kindertransport took them by boat to Britain.

**First kindertransport**
These excited Jewish refugee children are arriving in Harwich, England, on December 2, 1938, on the first kindertransport from Germany. At the time, they had no idea what the fate of their families would be back home. Following their arrival, many would board trains to communities where British families awaited them. Families from all over Britain, mostly non-Jewish, generously volunteered to look after refugee children at their own expense until the end of the war.

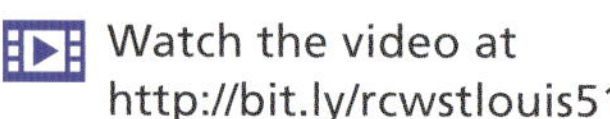
Watch the video at http://bit.ly/rcwstlouis51

REGISTRATION CERTIFICATE No. 902097.

ISSUED AT Cambridge Borough

ON - 4 NOV 1940

NAME·(Surname first in Roman Capitals)

MEIER ~~LÖWENSTEIN~~, Grete

ALIAS ~~LOEWENSTEIN~~, Greta

Left Thumb Print (if unable to sign name in English Characters).

ALIENS DEPARTMENT - 4 NOV 1940

PHOTOGRAPH

Signature of Holder. } Greta Loewenstein

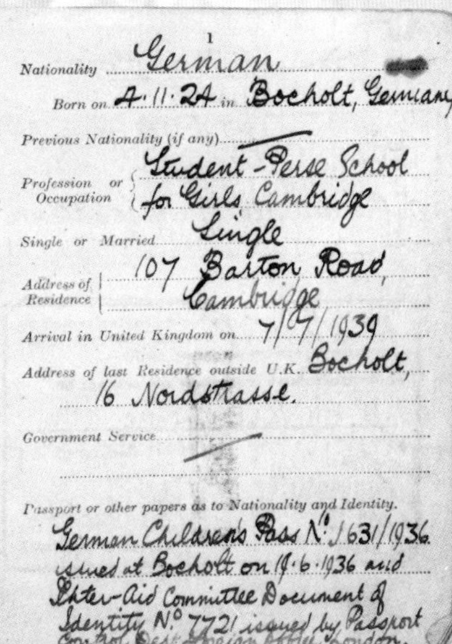

1

Nationality German

Born on 4·11·24 in Bocholt, Germany

Previous Nationality (if any) —

Profession or Occupation { Student - Perse School for Girls Cambridge

Single or Married Single

Address of Residence { 107 Barton Road, Cambridge

Arrival in United Kingdom on 7/7/1939

Address of last Residence outside U.K. Bocholt, 16 Nordstrasse.

Government Service —

Passport or other papers as to Nationality and Identity.

German Children's Pass No. 1631/1936 issued at Bocholt on 19·6·1936 and Inter-Aid Committee Document of Identity No. 7721 issued by Passport Control Dept. Foreign Office, London.

**A new life in England**

Grete Loewenstein came to England on a kindertransport in July 1939. She was issued this certificate of registration and then sent to live with a British family for the duration of the war. Like most of the children who were evacuated from Europe, Grete expected the war to end quickly and to be reunited with her parents soon. Sadly, many of their families did not survive the war.

**Bombing in England**

These children sit on what is left of their home after it was bombed in London, England. Between September 1940 and May 1941, the German Air Force mounted a series of bombing raids on a number of British cities and ports, including London. The bombings became known as "the Blitz," which is the German word for "lightning" since the night skies were lit up by the explosions. Over 40,000 civilians were killed, and thousands of children were evacuated to the English countryside.

**Evacuated again**

These young Jewish refugees came to England on a kindertransport. They were initially housed in a B'nai Brith hostel in Hackney, London. Although they had narrowly escaped death in Germany, they still faced the dangers of war. London was heavily bombed by the Germans between September 1940 and May 1941. These girls were evacuated to the English countryside and are pictured here in Swaffham, Norfolk, in September 1940.

## CHAPTER 3

# ANTI-SEMITISM IN CANADA

## Racism on the Rise

Canada's anti-Semitism increased with the rise of fascism in Europe. During the 1920s and 30s, Jews in Canada were barred from many public places including beaches, hotels and resorts. Many neighbourhoods prohibited Jews from buying homes. Signs reading "No Jews or dogs allowed" or "Gentiles only" were posted in the Beaches in Toronto and in other neighbourhoods. Some professions were closed to Jews. In Toronto, the 1933 Christie Pits Riot brought increased attention to the rising anti-Semitism spreading across the country.

TORONTO DAILY STAR

TORONTO, THURSDAY, APRIL 13, 1933

COATSWORTH HAD LETTER SENT OUT IN TINKER'S NAME

Admits He Had No Legal Right to Interfere in Leaside Case

"TRYING TO HELP"

CAMPAIGN AGAINST JEWS HIGHLY ORGANIZED IN BERLIN

DIVORCE IS GRANTED UPON NEW EVIDEN[illegible]

Justice Rose Reverses Ju[illegible] ment in Brooke Case

BOY, TIRED FR[illegible] BURNED [illegible]

Two Small Sisters and L[illegible]

**Nazis in the news**
As early as 1933, Canadian newspapers, like this one, were reporting on the Nazi campaign against Jews in Germany. Canadians were aware of the increasing Jewish persecution overseas.

**Adrien Arcand**
The leading Canadian fascist of the 1930s and 40s was Adrien Arcand, pictured here. He was a francophone journalist based in Montreal, a fierce anti-Semite and an admirer of Hitler and other fascist leaders around the world. He led the Parti National Social Chrétien du Canada (PSNC), which proudly displayed the swastika, the symbol of the Nazi Party.

VOTEZ POUR

**Symbol of hate**
The use of the swastika as a symbol of anti-Semitism in Quebec in the 1930s can be attributed to Arcand and his party. This image shows a key with the swastika and slogan, "La clef du nouveau Canada." The translation is "The key to a new Canada."

**Neighbourhood complaints**
When local Jewish community members held a picnic at Toronto's eastern beaches, some of the neighbours complained. They called it a "foreign invasion" and eventually posted signs saying "no dogs or Jews allowed."

Anti-Jewish signs sprang up across Ontario in the 1930s.

**Anti-Semitic sign**
Many anti-Jewish signs, like this one, sprang up across Ontario in the 1930s. The word "Gentile" means a person who is not a Jew. Unlike today, discrimination and racism was not illegal then.

**Swastika Club**

The swastika, seen on the shirt on the right, was adopted by Adolf Hitler for his Nazi party and became a symbol of fascism in Canada too. Fascism attracted many supporters during the 1930s. The Swastika Club of Toronto, a group of anti-Jewish people in the eastern beaches, organized parades on the boardwalk in their neighbourhood to discourage Jewish visitors to the area. Club members, many sporting swastika emblems on their shirts, taunted and intimidated Jews who came to enjoy the parkland and beaches there.

WATCH THE VIDEO

**The Christie Pits Riot**

On August 16, 1933, a riot erupted following a baseball game at Christie Pits, Toronto. Trouble between Jews and fascists had been brewing for some time. Earlier in the month, this swastika and slogan appeared on the clubhouse roof at the ball park. The conflict came to blows when a large swastika symbol was unveiled at the end of the ball game. Hundreds of people were injured, but nobody was killed. Although the police had been warned about trouble, they did nothing to prevent it.

Watch the video at http://bit.ly/rcwstlouis03

The Mail and Empire.

SCORES HURT AS SWASTIKA MOBS RIOT AT WILLOWVALE

MAYOR PROMISES IMMEDIATE PROBE OF DISTURBANCES

Thousands Caught Up in Park Melee Gangs Wielding Lead Pipes and Bats Sweep Streets, Bludgeoning Victims

The Mail and Empire.

BALMY BEACH DANCE HALL CLOSED TO AVERT SWASTIKA ROW

"Nazi" Parade Tours Boardwalk Singing Anti-Jewish Doggerel

Temperature Tumbles But Toronto Is Robbed Of Relief by Humidity

Police Called in as Noisy Throngs Threaten Disturbance at Canoe Club

Hitler Emblems Stir Jewish Protest

THE TORONTO DAILY STAR

SWASTIKA CLUB WILL GIVE UP EMBLEM

HOME AND SPORT EDITION

The Daily Hebrew Journal

דער אידישער זשורנאל

**Headlines**

The Christie Pits riot was the topic of headlines for days after the violence. The growing problem of anti-Semitism in Toronto could no longer be ignored by officials. Note the newspaper on the bottom is written in Yiddish, the language spoken by Eastern European Jews.

Canadian Jews formed anti-fascist leagues across the country.

**Swastika ban**
Toronto Mayor William J. Stewart, pictured here, became a hero to many in the Jewish community by banning the public display of the swastika in the aftermath of the riot.

AVIS

Les Juifs ne sont pas désirés ici, Ste-Agathe est un village canadien français et nous le garderons ainsi.

NOTICE

Jews are not wanted here in Ste. Agathe, so scram while the going is good.

**Anti-Semitism in Quebec**
This anti-Semitic sign was posted in the Quebec village of Sainte Agathe-des-Monts in July 1939.

**Jewish anti-fascist leagues**
Canadian Jews watched with alarm the rise of fascism in Europe. Newspapers reported on the growing violence against Jews, particularly in Germany. Canadian Jews formed anti-fascist leagues across the country and urged politicians to stop the growing anti-Semitic propaganda spread by fascists. This stamp, urging the boycott of German-made goods, was distributed by the Jewish Anti-Fascist League of Winnipeg in 1938.

# Canada Closes its Doors

After the First World War, Canada and many other countries around the world were hit hard by an economic depression. In the 1930s, many people were out of work, and Canadians were especially afraid of new immigrants taking away their jobs. Anti-Semitism and anti-immigrant sentiments were increasing across the country, fueled by the desire to keep Canada a white Anglo-Saxon country and in Quebec, to maintain the Roman Catholic majority. These attitudes led to passage of restrictive immigration laws that closed Canada's doors to most Jews. Between January and November 1938, the cost for a Jewish family to enter Canada tripled from $5,000 to $15,000. In September 1938, Frederick Blair, Director of Immigration, sent a letter to Prime Minister Mackenzie King stating, "Pressure by Jewish people to get into Canada has never been greater than it is now, and I am glad to be able to add that, after 35 years of experience here, it has never been so carefully controlled."

**HAND PICKED ONLY**
**JACK CANUCK: I want settlers, but will accept no culls.**

**Hand-picked only**
In 1919, the Canadian government passed legislation allowing it to rate potential immigrants based on their race, nationality and occupation. British and Americans were rated at the top of the list while Jews, Asians, Romani and Black people were at the bottom. This cartoon caption reads, "Jack Canuck: I want settlers, but will accept no culls [inferior people that nobody else wants]." In other words, Canada wanted immigrants but only those they considered desirable.

## Restrictive immigration laws closed Canada's doors to most Jews.

**Frederick Charles Blair**
Frederick Charles Blair joined Canada's immigration office in 1905, became the assistant deputy minister in 1924 and took over as director from 1936 to 1943. He was anti-Semitic and racist. During the 1930s, when the Great Depression left thousands of Canadians unemployed, the government restricted immigration even more. Very few Jews, except for farmers and wealthy individuals, were permitted into the country. Blair was proud of his selective policies. In his 1941 annual report he wrote, "Canada, in accordance with generally accepted practice, places greater emphasis on race than upon citizenship."

**The lucky ones**
This group of Slovak and Hungarian Jewish families were among the few Jews accepted to Canada during the 1930s. Nandor and Magda Muller, pictured above, lived a comfortable life in Czechoslovakia until 1939, when the fascist movement turned violent against the Jewish population. In order to get their visas to Canada, the Mullers had to pledge to live in a rural area or take up farming. They left Slovakia with their two children in late August 1939, just prior to the outbreak of the Second World War, and settled on a farm in Thorold, Ontario.

**Muller children**
Alice and Heinrich Muller came to Canada with their parents in 1939, barely escaping the horrors about to engulf Europe.

# Fight for Immigration

The rise of Nazism in Germany was making the situation desperate for Jews trying to leave that country. Jewish groups, such as the Canadian Jewish Congress (CJC), tried to get the government to open doors to Jewish immigrants but anti-Semitism in the Department of Immigration and the general public blocked their efforts. As a result, Jewish refugees were treated differently than other Europeans seeking entry into Canada. When asked how many Jews should be admitted, Frederick Blair, Director of Immigration, answered, "None is too many."

On March 29, 1938, Prime Minister Mackenzie King wrote in his private diary, "We must nevertheless seek to keep this part of the Continent free from unrest and from too great an intermixture of foreign strains of blood, as much the same thing as lies at the basis of the Oriental problem. I fear we would have riots if we agreed to a policy that admitted numbers of Jews."

**The Canadian Jewish Congress**
The CJC was founded in 1919 to provide assistance to Eastern European Jews in Canada. During its first few years, the organization unified Canadian Jewry and established the Jewish Immigrant Aid Society. It also acted as the main advocacy group for Canada's Jewish community. As fear grew about the safety of Jews in Nazi Germany, the CJC took action. In 1934, above, they met in Toronto to organize increased lobbying of officials to allow more Jewish immigrants into Canada. They also promoted campaigns to fight Nazis abroad and anti-Semitism at home. Part of their efforts were focused on urging Britain to open up Palestine to Jews trying to flee Nazi Germany.

**Lillian Freiman**
Lillian Freiman was a vigilant worker on behalf of Jewish immigrants to Canada. She also fought for the establishment of a Jewish homeland in Palestine and founded the Canadian Hadassah, a Jewish women's charitable organization.

**Samuel Bronfman**
Samuel Bronfman, pictured here in 1939, was the son of early Jewish settlers in Wapella, Saskatchewan. His family had very successful businesses in Montreal and was actively involved in Jewish philanthropy. He took over as president of the CJC in 1938. He fought hard to get Canada to accept more Jewish refugees from Europe.

**Canada let them down**
In 1941, the Canadian Jewish community lobbied the government to allow the rescue of Jewish orphans in France. The Canadian parliament was very slow to respond. When they finally agreed to initially allow 500 orphans from Vichy, France, to come to Canada, and another 500 at a later date, it was too late. The orphans, some of whom are pictured above, were captured by the Germans and sent to concentration camps where many did not survive.

**Bora Laskin**
Bora Laskin was a child of Russian immigrants who grew up in Fort William (Thunder Bay), Ontario. He became a Toronto lawyer and a member of the Legal Affairs Committee of CJC. He took the lead in fighting bigotry and racism throughout the country and fought Canada's anti-Jewish immigration laws. In later years, Mr. Laskin became Canada's first Jewish Chief Justice.

# CHAPTER 4
# MS *ST. LOUIS*

## Ship of Hope

Hitler originally wanted all Jews to leave Germany. Initially, Jews were reluctant to leave their homes and businesses. Many families had lived in Germany for over two hundred years. Jewish men fought for Germany in the First World War and considered themselves loyal Germans. They couldn't believe the country would turn on them. Once danger became apparent, those who wanted to leave could not get visas for other countries, so they purchased landing visas from the Cuban embassy. They planned to stay in Cuba while their applications for the US were processed. The MS *St. Louis* was a German ocean luxury liner. It left Hamburg, Germany, for Cuba on May 13, 1939, carrying 937 Jewish refugees, including hundreds of children.

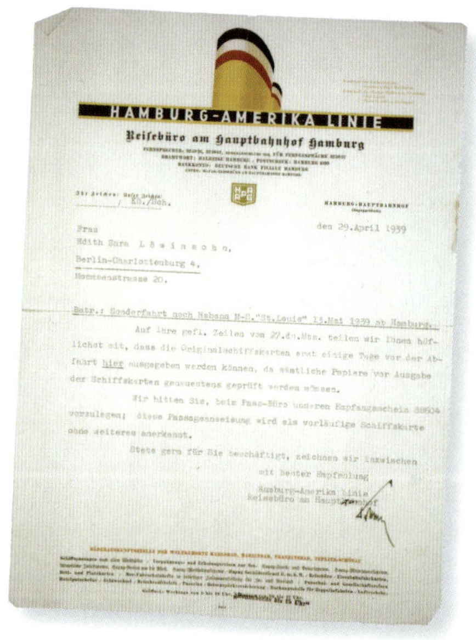

HAMBURG-AMERIKA LINIE
Reisebüro am Hauptbahnhof Hamburg

Frau
Edith Sara Löwinsohn,
Berlin-Charlottenburg 4,

den 29. April 1939

Betr.: Sonderfahrt nach Habana M-S. "St. Louis" 13. Mai 1939 ab Hamburg.

Auf Ihre gefl. Zeilen vom 27.d.Mts. teilen wir Ihnen höflichst mit, dass die Originalschiffskarten erst einige Tage vor der Abfahrt hier ausgegeben werden können, da sämtliche Papiere vor Ausgabe der Schiffskarten gewissenhaft geprüft werden müssen.

Wir bitten Sie, beim Pass-Büro unseren Empfangsschein vorzulegen; diese Passageanweisung wird als vorläufige Schiffskarte ohne weiteres anerkannt.

Stets gern für Sie beschäftigt, zeichnen wir inzwischen

mit bester Empfehlung

Hamburg-Amerika Linie
Reisebüro am Hauptbahnhof

**Booking passage**
This letter from a travel agency to Edith Loewensohn, dated April 29, 1939, confirmed her passage on the MS *St. Louis*.

## The Route of the *St. Louis*, May 13–June 17, 1939

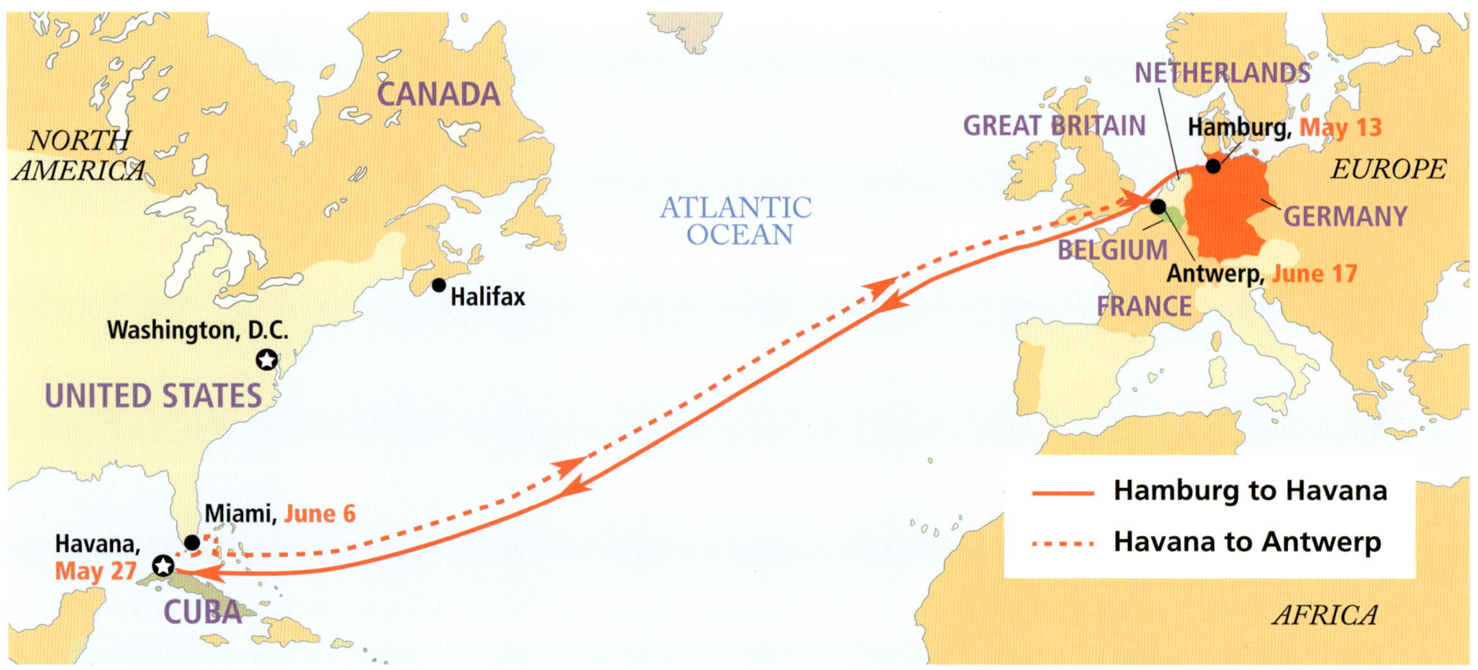

**MS *St. Louis***
The MS *St. Louis*, pictured on this postcard, was part of the Hamburg-America Line of ships. It was a large, well-built ship with many luxurious features for its time. Many thousands of Jewish people fled Germany while they still could. Most of the 937 passengers were German Jews, but a few were from eastern Europe, Spain and Cuba. Most had lost their businesses and homes due to the widespread persecution of Jews. Some of the male passengers had been released from concentration camps in Dachau and Buchenwald with the condition that they leave Germany immediately.

WATCH THE VIDEO

**Boys on board**
Six-year-old Gerald Granston, above on the right, recalled his reaction when his father told him they were leaving Germany for the other side of the world. "I'd never heard of Cuba and I couldn't imagine what was going to happen. I remember being scared all the time."

Watch the video at http://bit.ly/rcwstlouis04

**High hopes**
Like many of the youth on the *St. Louis*, Walter Karliner appears excited about the voyage as he awaits departure from Hamburg in May 1939.

**Leaving Hamburg**
The *St. Louis* is pictured here leaving Hamburg in May 1939. Most of the passengers had bought landing visas for Cuba. They had also filled out applications to continue on to America where many had families. They were not planning to stay in Cuba.

**Captain Gustav Schroeder**
Gustav Schroeder was the ship's captain. He ordered his staff to treat the passengers with dignity and respect, unlike how they were treated at home in Germany. He allowed traditional Friday night prayers on board, even taking down the portrait of Hitler hanging in the main dining room.

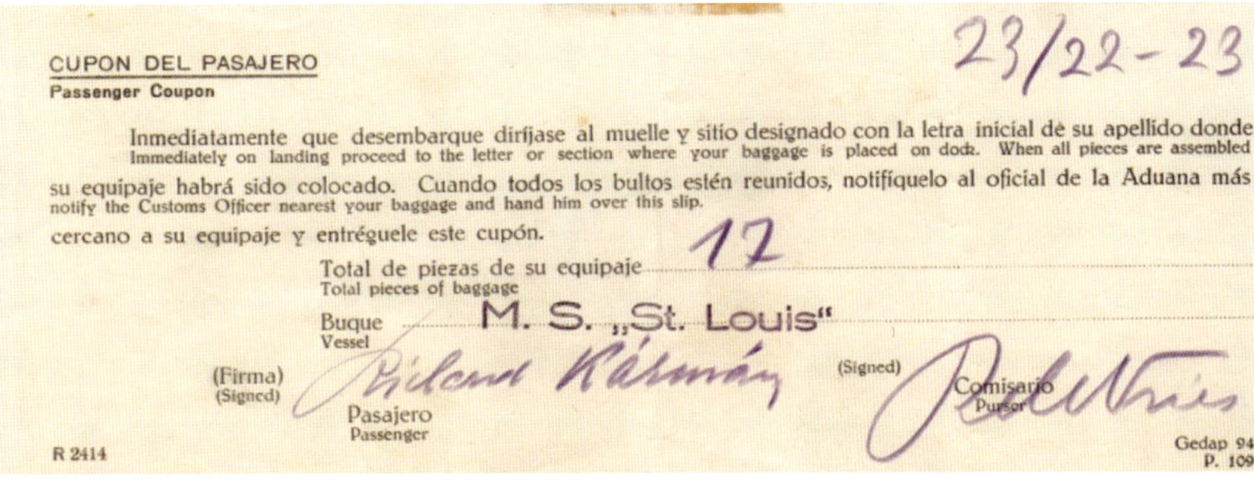
CUPON DEL PASAJERO
Passenger Coupon

23/22-23

Inmediatamente que desembarque diríjase al muelle y sitio designado con la letra inicial de su apellido donde su equipaje habrá sido colocado. Cuando todos los bultos estén reunidos, notifíquelo al oficial de la Aduana más cercano a su equipaje y entréguele este cupón.
Immediately on landing proceed to the letter or section where your baggage is placed on dock. When all pieces are assembled notify the Customs Officer nearest your baggage and hand him over this slip.

Total de piezas de su equipaje / Total pieces of baggage: 17

Buque / Vessel: M. S. „St. Louis"

(Firma) (Signed) Richard Kármán
Pasajero / Passenger

(Signed) Comisario / Purser

R 2414

Gedap 94
P. 109

**Passenger coupon**
The Karman family was issued this passenger coupon for the MS *St. Louis* in order to claim their luggage and pass through customs upon arrival in Cuba.

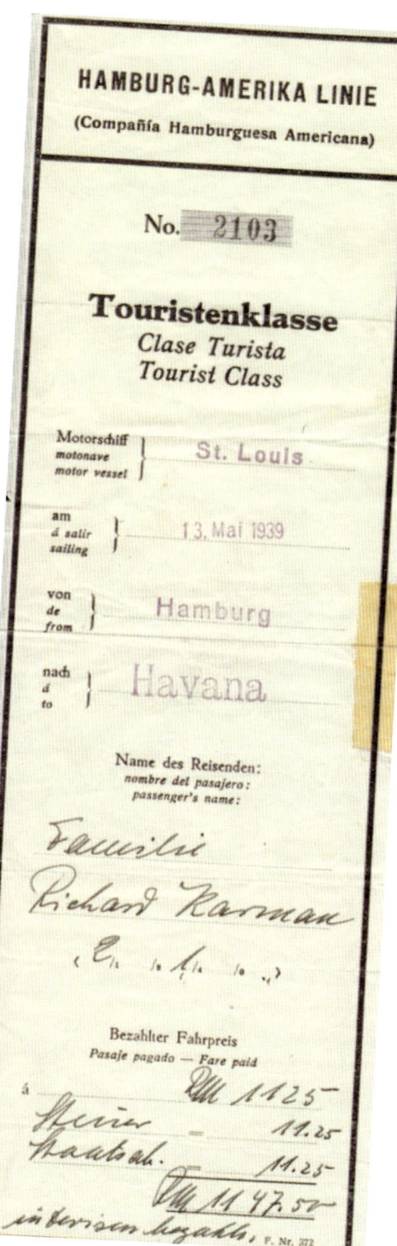
HAMBURG-AMERIKA LINIE
(Compañía Hamburguesa Americana)

No. 2103

Touristenklasse
Clase Turista
Tourist Class

Motorschiff / motonave / motor vessel: St. Louis
am / á salir / sailing: 13. Mai 1939
von / de / from: Hamburg
nach / á / to: Havana

Name des Reisenden: / nombre del pasajero: / passenger's name:
Familie
Richard Karman

Bezahlter Fahrpreis
Pasaje pagado — Fare paid
RM 1125–
Steuer – 11.25
Staatsab. 11.25
RM 1147.50
in Devisen bezahlt. F. Nr. 372

**Ticket for the "Ship of Hope"**
Ticket for passage on the MS *St. Louis* for Richard Karman, his wife, Sidonia, and their four-year-old daughter, Ana Maria.

**Karman family**
Richard Karman is pictured here in the background wearing a hat, sunglasses and shorts. He and his wife, Sidonia, were traveling to America with their small daughter, Ana Maria.

**Ana Maria Karman**
Ana Maria Karman was four years old when she crossed the Atlantic Ocean on the MS *St. Louis* with her parents. She recalls, "I was just a kid but I remember that we were very happy on board. I played with other children. My parents told me that I was the only one who didn't get lost on the ship."

# Life on Board

At first the passengers on board the ship enjoyed the voyage. Children played on deck and splashed in the ship's swimming pool. Passengers gathered in the dining room for meals. There were movies and music and dancing. Everyone was happy to be out of Germany. Ursula and Eric Spitz were looking forward to reuniting with their father who had gone ahead to Cuba earlier in the year.

**Early arrival**
As conditions for Jews worsened in Germany, businessman George Spitz, pictured here, chose what seemed to be the best option to get his family out of the country. He bought visas from the Cuban government for himself, his wife, Vera, and his two teenaged children, Ursula and Eric. At the end of April 1939, George sailed to Cuba ahead of the family to find a job and a place to live. He also prepared for his family's arrival. Upon landing in Cuba, George's visa was accepted, and he was allowed to enter the country. His goal was for the family to stay in Cuba while applying for entry into the United States.

**Ursula Spitz**
Ursula, nicknamed Uschi, was sixteen years old when she set sail with her mother and brother on the *St. Louis*.

**Leaving it all behind**
The Spitz family lived in Breslau, Germany. It is now part of western Poland and is called Wrocław. Vera and her husband knew they had to escape the mounting violence against Jews, so they agreed to leave their home and extended family to begin a new life in America. First they had to get to Cuba. Since her husband had gone ahead, Vera was alone with her two teenagers on board the *St. Louis*.

**A happy time at sea**
Fourteen-year-old Eric Spitz (circled) attends a dinner party for the younger crowd on the *St. Louis.*

**Relaxing on deck**
Uschi Spitz sits on a lounge chair and chats with another passenger.

## Children played on deck and splashed in the ship's swimming pool. There were movies and music and dancing.

**Dining room**
Life in Germany had been very stressful and unstable for many of the passengers. On board the ship, they were given beautiful meals with a variety of food that they had not seen in Germany for a while. Each evening a dance band played. There was also a cinema on board.

**Dressed for dinner**
Passengers on board dressed up for their evening meals and entertainment. These young men look very happy with their life on board the ship.

"It was really something to be going on a luxury liner."
–15-year-old Gisela Feldman

**Teenaged passengers**
Fifteen-year-old Gisela Feldman recalled how she felt about the voyage. "It was really something to be going on a luxury liner. We didn't know where we were heading or how we would cope when we got there. I was always aware of how anxious my mother looked, embarking on such a long journey, on her own with two teenage daughters." Gisela said she spent her time on board walking around the deck, chatting with boys her own age or swimming in the ship's pool.

WATCH THE VIDEO

**Children**
Hundreds of young children accompanied their parents on the *St. Louis*. Their smiling faces reflect their ease and excitement to be on such an adventure. Six-year-old Sol Messinger recalled being repeatedly told by adults that they were safe now. "We don't have to look over our shoulders anymore," they would say.

Watch the video at http://bit.ly/rcwstlouis52

# Arrival in Cuba

When the *St. Louis* arrived in Havana Harbor on May 27, 1939, the Cuban government only admitted 28 passengers: 22 of them were Jewish and had valid US visas; the remaining six — four Spanish citizens and two Cuban nationals — had valid entry documents. One further passenger was evacuated to a hospital in Havana after attempting to commit suicide. Corrupt Cuban officials demanded more money and then refused to recognize the refugees' visas. The passengers were forced to stand on deck and look at the shoreline of the country they had thought would be their refuge. For several days, Captain Schroeder and officials from the American Jewish Joint Distribution Committee (JDC) tried to negotiate with Cuba's President Federico Bru. As the passengers' hopes were dashed, mood on board became tense. Finally, on June 2, President Bru ordered the Captain to take the ship out of Cuban waters.

**At ease**
Life on board a luxury liner in the warm sunshine was a great contrast to the hostilities that Uschi and her family had left behind in Germany. Here, she and another passenger enjoy the warm weather as they sail closer to Cuba.

**Havana Harbor**
As the ship approached Cuba, the passengers became more excited about their new freedom ahead. They arrived in Havana Harbor on May 27, 1939. Here, passengers are seen on board with the city of Havana visible in the background.

"The Cuban government is forcing us to leave the port." — Capt. Schroeder

**Confined to the ship**

Instead of disembarking in Havana, most of the passengers found themselves confined to the ship. In this image, passengers are trying to communicate with friends and relatives who had arrived in Cuba before them, when Cuba was still accepting Jewish refugees. The greeters were allowed to approach the docked vessel, but they could not board the *St. Louis*. Vera Spitz and her children stood at the rail and waved to George, who was in a small boat. Once the Cuban officials refused landing, Jewish organizations were contacted and they began negotiating on behalf of the passengers.

**Forced to leave**

On June 1, 1939, Captain Schroeder read this message to his passengers. The translated text reads: "The Cuban government is forcing us to leave the port. They have permitted us to stay here until daybreak and the departure is set for 10:00 Friday morning. The departure has not brought about any disruption in the negotiations. Only the situation brought about by the departure of the ship is a precondition for the intervention of Mr. Berenson and his co-workers. The ship administration will remain in further contact with all Jewish organizations and all other governmental offices, and will, with all available means, seek a remedy, so that a disembarkation outside Germany will occur, and we will stay for the time being near the American coast."

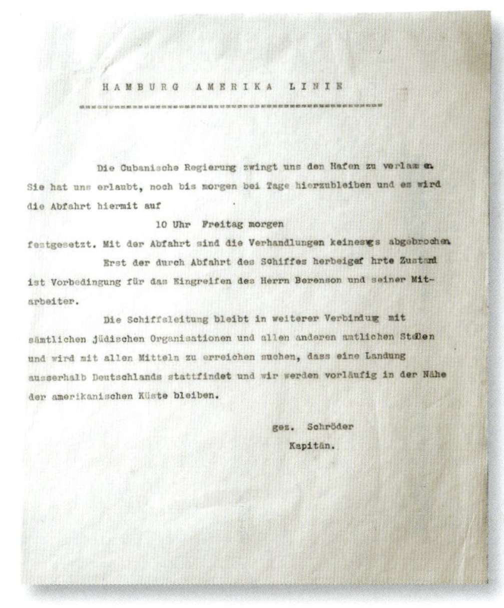

H A M B U R G   A M E R I K A   L I N I E

Die Cubanische Regierung zwingt uns den Hafen zu verlassen. Sie hat uns erlaubt, noch bis morgen bei Tage hierzubleiben und es wird die Abfahrt hiermit auf

10 Uhr Freitag morgen

festgesetzt. Mit der Abfahrt sind die Verhandlungen keineswegs abgebrochen.

Erst der durch Abfahrt des Schiffes herbeigef hrte Zustand ist Vorbedingung für das Eingreifen des Herrn Berenson und seiner Mitarbeiter.

Die Schiffsleitung bleibt in weiterer Verbindung mit sämtlichen jüdischen Organisationen und allen anderen amtlichen Stellen und wird mit allen Mitteln zu erreichen suchen, dass eine Landung ausserhalb Deutschlands stattfindet und wir werden vorläufig in der Nähe der amerikanischen Küste bleiben.

gez. Schröder
Kapitän.

**Child's drawing**

Liesl Joseph, an eleven-year-old passenger, drew this picture of the ship. Her father, Josef, was the chairman of the passenger committee that tried to find a safe place for the ship to land. Liesl remembered thinking, "As long as my father was involved, we would be all right."

# Searching for Safety

The Captain sailed toward Miami, Florida, in hopes that the US would allow the refugees to enter the country. They were so close to shore that passengers could see the lights of the city. When American officials refused to admit the refugees, Captain Schroeder headed north. On June 7, 41 prominent Canadian citizens petitioned Prime Minister Mackenzie King to provide sanctuary for the refugees. King, who was away on official business, turned the matter over to Director of Immigration Frederick Blair who in turn refused to give them asylum. Captain Schroeder refused to return the ship to Nazi Germany, but he had no choice but to sail back to Europe. After much negotiation, four countries agreed to take them: Britain, France, Belgium and the Netherlands.

**Rejected by the United States**
When negotiations with the Cuban authorities fell apart, the next step was to ask the US to accept the ship and its passengers. On June 2, 1939, the ship left Cuba and sailed toward the Florida coastline. Passengers recalled seeing the lights of Miami at night. The *St. Louis* was met by the American coast guard who prevented them from getting closer to shore. The passenger committee, along with many American groups and individuals, appealed to President Franklin D. Roosevelt to allow the refugees to land. The president refused. This painting by Sol Levenson shows Uncle Sam, a symbol of the US, shoving the *St. Louis* into the flaming mouth of Adolf Hitler.

**Canada says "No"**
When the US refused to take the passengers, the *St. Louis* headed north. Word of the refugees' desperate situation reached Canada, and people quickly organized a campaign for their acceptance. On June 7, a delegation petitioned Prime Minister Mackenzie King. He left the decision to Director of Immigration Frederick Blair (above left). Blair is quoted as saying, "No country could open its doors wide enough to take in the hundreds of thousands of Jewish people who want to leave Europe; the line must be drawn somewhere." The ship was only two days sail away from Halifax Harbour when the captain received word that it could not land in Canada.

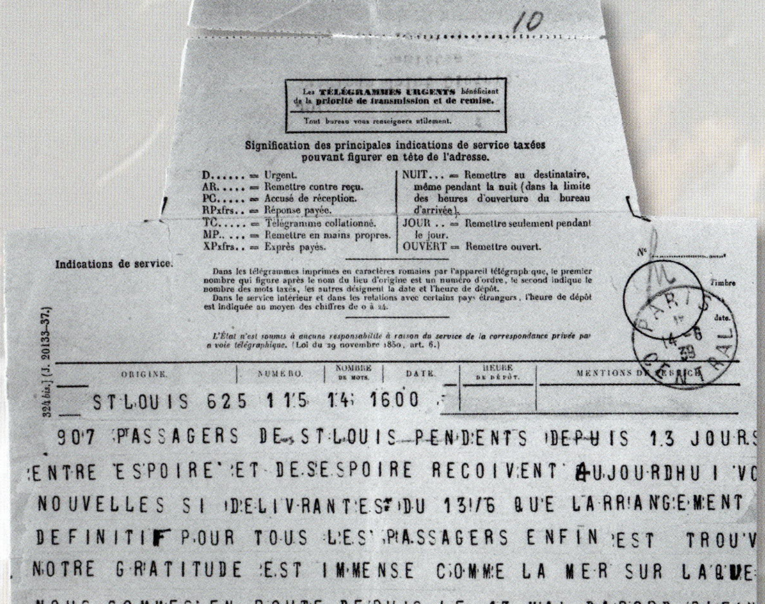

10

Les TÉLÉGRAMMES URGENTS bénéficient de la priorité de transmission et de remise.

Tout bureau vous renseignera utilement.

Signification des principales indications de service taxées pouvant figurer en tête de l'adresse.

D...... = Urgent.
AR..... = Remettre contre reçu.
PC..... = Accusé de réception.
RPxfrs.. = Réponse payée.
TC..... = Télégramme collationné.
MP..... = Remettre en mains propres.
XPxfrs.. = Exprès payés.

NUIT... = Remettre au destinataire, même pendant la nuit (dans la limite des heures d'ouverture du bureau d'arrivée).
JOUR .. = Remettre seulement pendant le jour.
OUVERT = Remettre ouvert.

Indications de service.

Dans les télégrammes imprimés en caractères romains par l'appareil télégraphique, le premier nombre qui figure après le nom du lieu d'origine est un numéro d'ordre, le second indique le nombre des mots taxés, les autres désignent la date et l'heure de dépôt.
Dans le service intérieur et dans les relations avec certains pays étrangers, l'heure de dépôt est indiquée au moyen des chiffres de 0 à 24.

*L'État n'est soumis à aucune responsabilité à raison du service de la correspondance privée par la voie télégraphique.* (Loi du 29 novembre 1850, art. 6.)

N°

Timbre à date.

PARIS CENTRAL 14-6 39

324 bis.] (J. 20133–37.)

| ORIGINE. | NUMÉRO. | NOMBRE DE MOTS. | DATE. | HEURE DE DÉPÔT. | MENTIONS DE SERVICE |
|---|---|---|---|---|---|
| ST LOUIS | 625 | 115 | 14 | 1600 | |

907 PASSAGERS DE ST LOUIS PENDENTS DEPUIS 13 JOURS
ENTRE ESPOIRE ET DESESPOIRE RECOIVENT AUJOURDHUI VO
NOUVELLES SI DELIVRANTES DU 13/6 QUE L ARRANGEMENT
DEFINITIF POUR TOUS LES PASSAGERS ENFIN EST TROUV
NOTRE GRATITUDE EST IMMENSE COMME LA MER SUR LAQUE
NOUS SOMMES EN ROUTE DEPUIS LE 13 MAI DABORD PLEIN

**Thank you**
When the ship was rejected by the US and Canada, Captain Schroeder had no choice but to turn back to Europe. Gisela Feldman recalled, "The joy had gone out of everything. No one was talking about what would happen now." Gerald Granston remembered seeing adults walking around crying in despair. But Morris Troper, Director of the American Jewish Joint Distribution Committee, managed to negotiate with four European countries to accept the passengers. In this telegram dated June 14, 1939, the passengers express their gratitude to him. The text of the French telegram reads, "907 *St. Louis* passengers who have been hanging between hope and despair for the past 13 days, today received your news … that definitive arrangements have been made for all the passengers. Our gratitude is as immense as the sea that we have been sailing on since May 13."

**Celebration on board**
These children are at a party on board the MS *St. Louis*, celebrating the fact that Belgium, France, Great Britain and the Netherlands agreed to take all the passengers.

# Return to Europe

On June 17, 1939, the *St. Louis* docked in Antwerp, Belgium. From there, the passengers dispersed to France, Britain and the Netherlands, or stayed in Belgium. For the time being, the *St. Louis* passengers were safe. Then, on September 1, 1939, Germany invaded Poland and the Second World War began. Within a few months, German armies overran most of Continental Europe. The refugees that had stayed there were in mortal danger once again.

**Heading back**
The MS *St. Louis* headed back to Europe after a month at sea. At the time, Europe, except for Germany, was still considered safe. It wasn't until September 1, 1939, that Germany invaded Poland and the Second World War officially began. This image shows the cover of a photo album belonging to teen passenger, Fritz Buff.

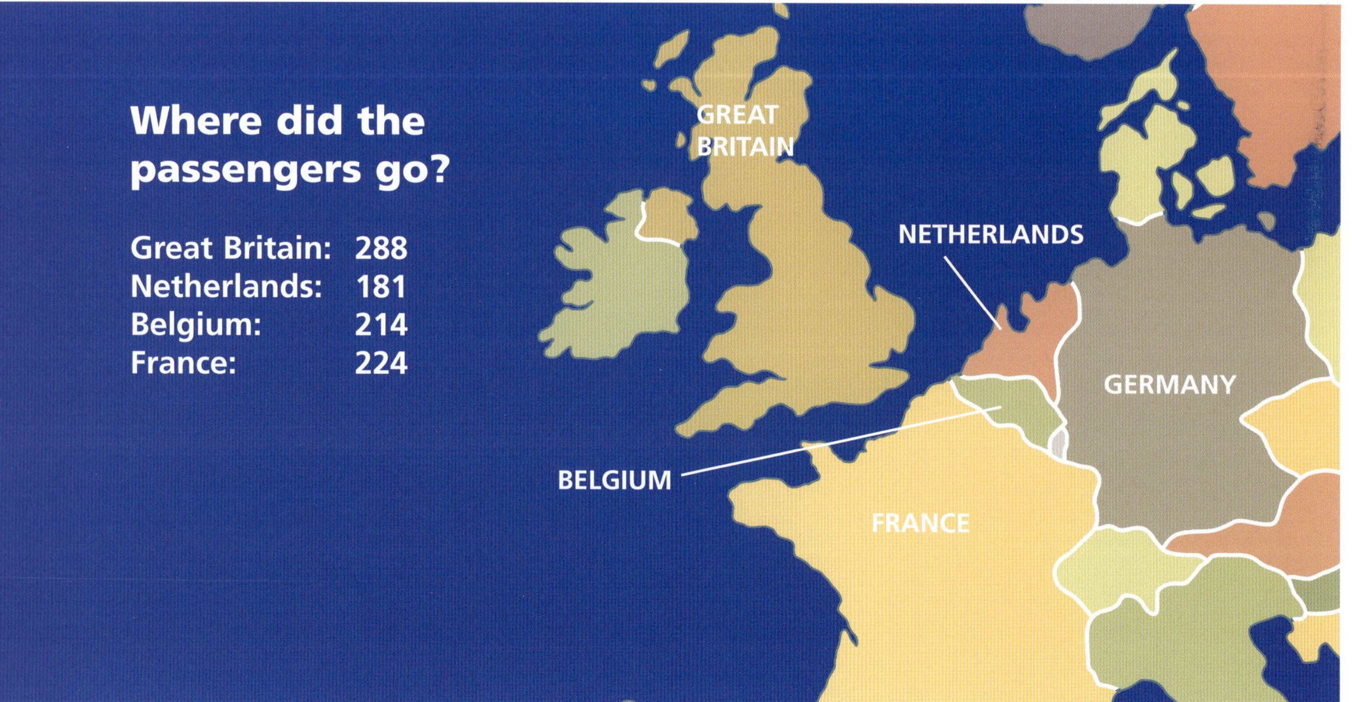


**Where did the passengers go?**

| | |
|---|---|
| Great Britain: | 288 |
| Netherlands: | 181 |
| Belgium: | 214 |
| France: | 224 |

**Landed in France**
This group of passengers from the *St. Louis* has just arrived in France after the ship returned to Europe. Although France was considered safe at the time, it would soon be occupied by the Nazis, and these refugees would once again be at their mercy.

**Arriving in Belgium**
The ship docked in Antwerp, Belgium on June 17, 1939. From there, passengers either stayed in Belgium or dispersed to the other three countries that would accept them. Gisela Feldman and Gerald Granston and their families went to Britain where they survived the war. Others weren't so lucky.

## The MS *St. Louis* headed back to Europe after a month at sea.

# Fate of the Passengers

Britain was the only one out of the four receptive countries that was not occupied by the Germans. The 288 refugees who went to Britain survived, except for one who was killed during a bombing raid over England. Most of the passengers who stayed in Continental Europe were captured by the invading German army and sent to concentration camps. Of them, 254 died in the Holocaust which lasted from 1941 to 1945. During the Holocaust, the Nazis murdered six million Jews and other targeted groups.

**Brief refuge**
After returning to Europe, the Karman family went to the Netherlands. Five-year-old Ana Maria Karman is pictured here in Amsterdam, where her family lived for a brief time. Her uncle lived in Mexico and sent them immigration papers, but it was too late. Germany invaded the Netherlands on May 10, 1940, and the family was trapped. They were captured and sent to the Westerbork concentration camp and then they were split up. Ana Maria and her mother were sent to Ravensbruck, and her father was sent to Buchenwald concentration camp. In March 1945, Ana Maria and her mother were liberated by the Swedish Red Cross and reunited with her father, who also survived. They moved to Mexico City where Ana Maria grew up. She now lives in Toronto, Ontario.

**Ravensbruck concentration camp**
Ana and her mother, Sidonia, were sent to Ravensbruck, a German concentration camp for females. Over 52,000 women and girls died there during the war.

**Buchenwald concentration camp**
Ana's father, Richard, was sent to Buchenwald in northern Germany. Most inmates worked as slave labourers. About 43,000 prisoners died there, and another 10,000 were shipped to extermination camps where they were murdered.

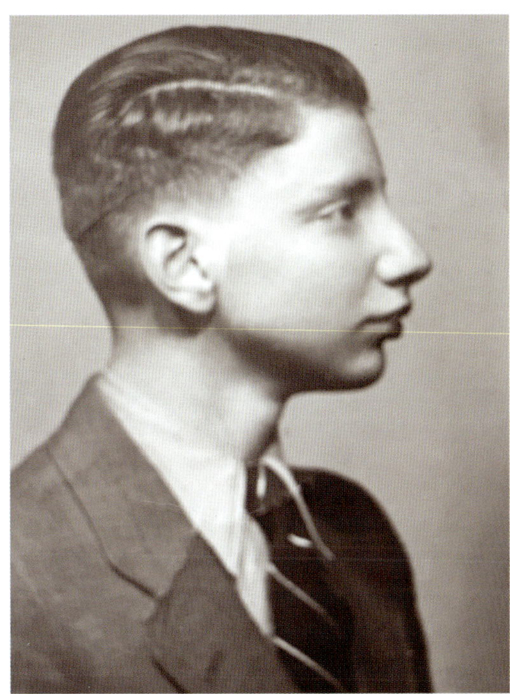

**Luckier than most**
When the passenger committee on the ship asked people which country they wanted to go to, Eric Spitz's family chose Britain. Of the four choices of countries, Britain was the only one that was not occupied by Germany during the war. In the summer of 1939, George Spitz joined his wife and children in London where they spent the war years. Eric, pictured here at 14, eventually joined the British army as a translator. He later immigrated to Canada.

**Bombing raid**
All of the 288 passengers who went directly to Great Britain survived the war except for one individual who was killed in a German bombing raid in 1940. The image on the right shows some of the damage caused by the bombing raids.

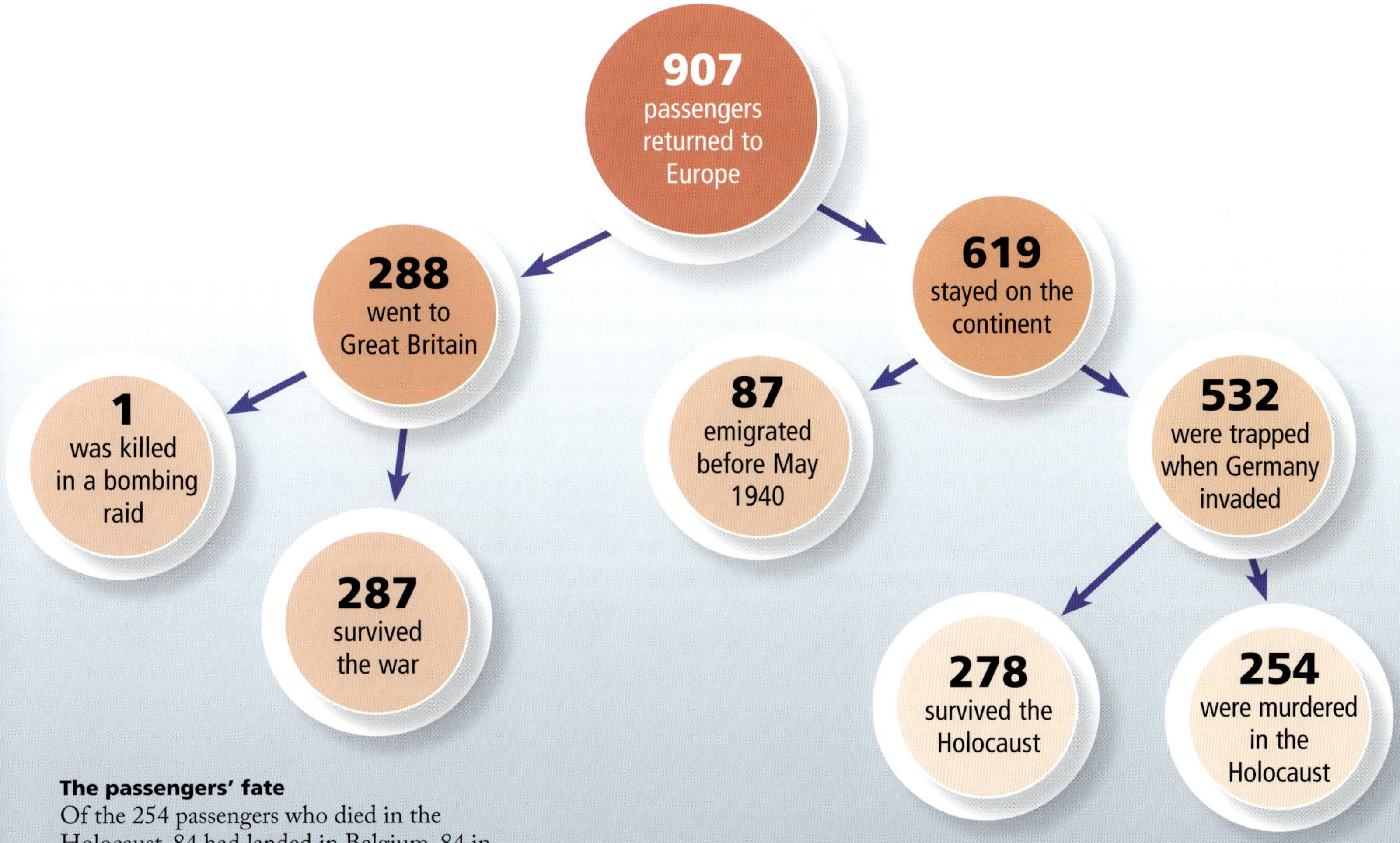

**907** passengers returned to Europe

**288** went to Great Britain

**1** was killed in a bombing raid

**287** survived the war

**619** stayed on the continent

**87** emigrated before May 1940

**532** were trapped when Germany invaded

**278** survived the Holocaust

**254** were murdered in the Holocaust

**The passengers' fate**
Of the 254 passengers who died in the Holocaust, 84 had landed in Belgium, 84 in the Netherlands and 86 in France.

# CHAPTER 5
# CANADA AT WAR, 1939–1945

## Canada Declares War

When Canada declared war on Germany in 1939, there were only 168,000 Jews living in Canada. From this relatively small community, over 17,000 Jewish-Canadian men and women served with the armed forces. They fought in all the major battles, including Dieppe, and the D-Day landings which began the Battle of Normandy. Two hundred were awarded medals for bravery, and 450 lost their lives fighting for peace and freedom.

**Canada at war**
Canada joined Britain in declaring war on Germany in September 1939, and then on Japan in December 1941. Men and women from across Canada volunteered to serve their country. Canadian troops fought in Europe and Japan, as part of the Allied forces.

**Sewing for the war effort**
This photo shows Canadian Jewish women volunteers sewing for the war effort in 1942. Women on the home front sewed quilts, bandages and clothing for the soldiers overseas.

**Jewish recruitment poster**
The Canadian Jewish Congress (CJC) issued this recruitment poster, calling on Canada's Jewish community to step up and do their part. Canadian Jews were active in the war effort, both in the armed forces and at home.

## Canadian Jews were active in the war effort, both in the armed forces and at home.

**Comic books**
To raise awareness of the contributions Canadian Jews were making to the war effort, the CJC produced these children's comics to tell stories of Jewish soldiers during the Second World War.

# Enemy Aliens

With the outbreak of war, the Canadian government passed the War Measures Act, which allowed the government to deny people's civil liberties, label them as enemy aliens and hold them in internment camps without any criminal charges. Internment camps were set up across the country from British Columbia to New Brunswick. Initially, known German-Canadian and other Canadian fascist sympathizers and German prisoners of war (POWs) sent from Britain were interned. A few hundred Italian-Canadians, mostly men accused of being fascists, were also interned. Once Canada was at war with Japan, all Japanese-Canadians living on the west coast, including children, were sent to internment camps. The camps were also used to intern innocent Jewish men and boys who were sent to Canada from Britain.

**Civil rights suspended**
Canada invoked the War Measures Act on August 25, 1939. It gave the government power to suspend the civil rights of people, including Canadian citizens. Canadian residents who were from enemy countries, or had roots in these countries could be declared enemy aliens. This came to include Germans, Italians and Japanese, as well as Jewish refugees from Europe. Here, an official is tacking up a poster announcing the legislation regarding the enemy alien status.

**Germans interned**
German Canadians suspected of Nazi party affiliations or members of German-sponsored organizations were rounded up and interned in camps such as Ripples, shown here in this painting by Oscar Bendl. Other known fascists, such as Canadian Adrien Arcand, were also interned. In addition, 700 German POWs were captured overseas and shipped to Canada for internment. In 1940, Jewish refugees would be interned here alongside their worst enemies.

**Italian-Canadians interned**
After Canada declared war on Italy in May 1940, approximately 600 Italian-Canadians were sent to internment camps. This model of Ripples, pictured above, is from the New Brunswick Internment Camp Museum in Minto, New Brunswick. Most of the interned Italian-Canadians were accused of being fascist supporters. Their stay in prison camp varied from a few months to years. None of the internees were ever charged with any wrongdoing.

**Japanese-Canadians interned in British Columbia**
As soon as Canada declared war on Japan following the attack on Pearl Harbor in December 1941, every Japanese-Canadian was declared an enemy alien. Nearly 22,000 Japanese-Canadian men, women and children in British Columbia were eventually forced into internment camps or into farm labour on the Prairies. This image shows the kind of shacks that families were forced to live in during internment in East Lillooet, British Columbia. No Japanese-Canadians were ever charged with any crimes.

# Jewish Refugees Interned in Canada

In the summer of 1940, Britain interned thousands of German and Austrian citizens who had fled to Britain, including Jewish refugees. They feared the possibility of a fifth column, or spies posing as refugees. Britain classified the internees into three categories: A) dangerous enemy aliens; and B) and C) — largely friendly and safe refugees. Britain asked Canada and Australia to take the B and C groups for the duration of the war. Canada only wanted to take the A group so that they could be locked up upon arrival. Instead, Britain sent them harmless refugees; 3,000 for the rest of the war. According to Alexander Paterson, British commissioner of prisons, sending the wrong refugees was a "gigantic and appalling mistake." Amongst the refugees were 2,300 German and Austrian Jews, some as young as fifteen years old. Britain told Canada to release them as friendly aliens, but Canada refused. Instead, Frederick Blair treated them as enemy aliens and put them in internment camps in Ontario, Quebec and New Brunswick. Initially, many of these Jewish refugees who had fled Nazi Germany were interned alongside German Nazi prisoners of war (POWs).

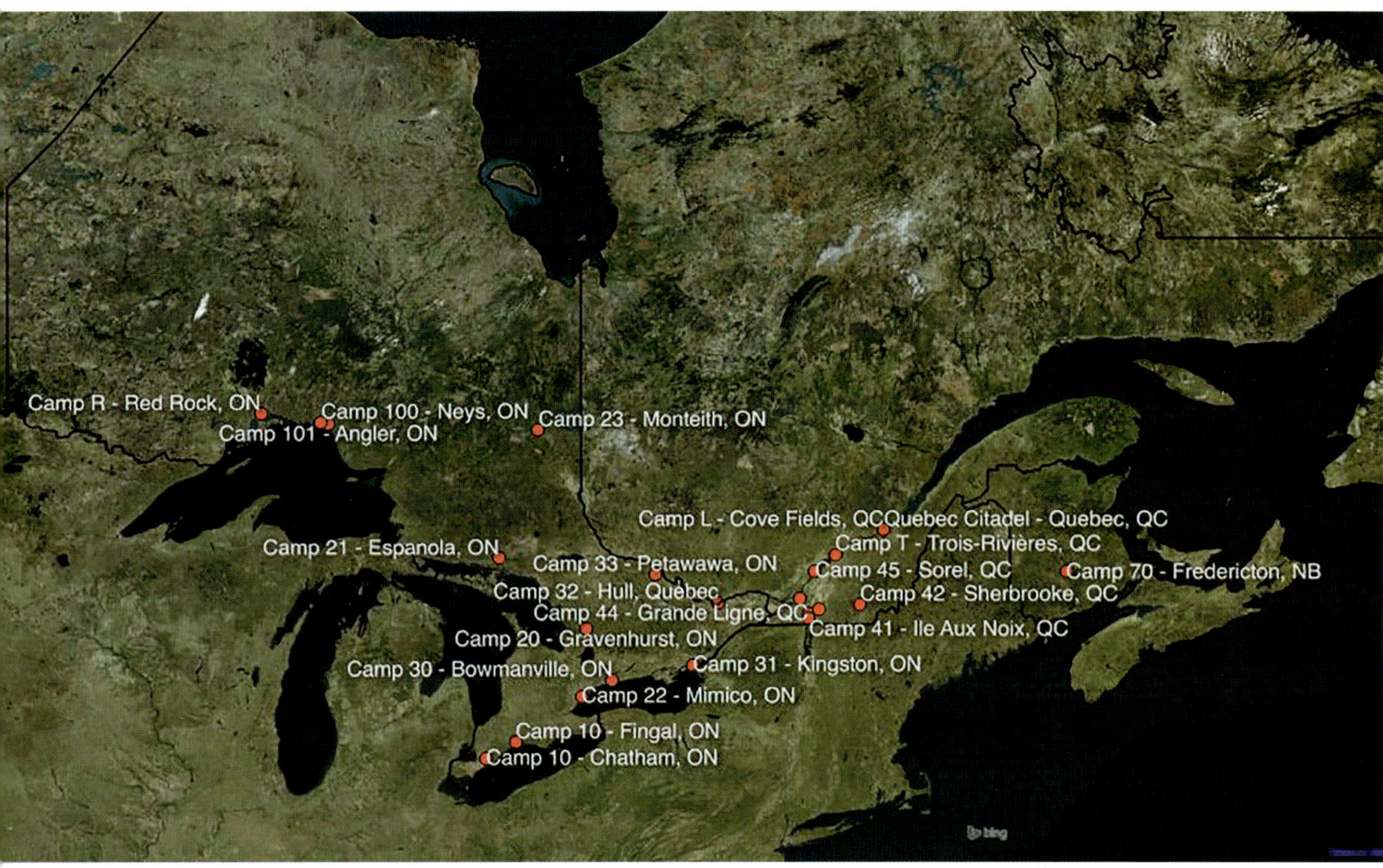


**Internment camps**
This map shows some of the internment camps in central and eastern Canada during the Second World War.

**Jewish refugee treated as an enemy alien**
In 1940, Edgar Lion, pictured here at age 98, was sent to Canada by Britain as part of a large group of Jewish refugees. He was born in Austria, but when he was 18 in 1938, his parents sent him to Britain to avoid the Nazi persecutions. Lion lived with a distant cousin in Edinburgh, Scotland, and took engineering at a local university. After the war started in May 1940, Britain rounded up all German and Austrian citizens and interned them as enemy aliens. Lion was sent to Huyton internment camp outside Liverpool, England, and then was forced on a ship. According to Lion, he was told to choose between two ships, not knowing where either one was headed. He ended up on a ship to Canada and was interned in Trois-Rivières, Quebec. The other ship went to Australia.

Watch the video at
http://bit.ly/rcwstlouis05

**Sent to New Brunswick camp**
Shortly after arriving in Quebec, Edgar Lion was moved to the Minto Internment camp in New Brunswick. This picture shows a model of the camp which is currently on display at the camp museum. Lion recalls, "The internment was one of the worst things for all of us because we didn't know what would happen to us in the future." Lion said, "We kept telling the authorities, 'We're on your side — we're with you!' But it didn't hold any water. They were afraid of spies and fifth columnists. It didn't matter that we were Jewish, that we were refugees from the Nazis. They just didn't want to accept it."

**Interned in Sherbrooke, Quebec**
After ten months in New Brunswick, Lion was sent to this camp in Sherbrooke, Quebec, where German POWs were also held. "There were real Nazis interned with us! They were Nazis who happened to be caught by the war in Great Britain. They were bragging and kept telling us, 'Wait till Hitler wins the war, we'll cut all your throats!'"

# Life in the Internment Camp

On August 12, 1940, 711 Jewish men and boys, some as young as fifteen, arrived in New Brunswick. They were interned in camp B70, Ripples, a small community about twenty kilometres outside of Fredericton, New Brunswick. They were German refugees who had gone to England to escape the Nazis, some on the kindertransports. When the Jews arrived at the camp, the German POWs hurled anti-Semitic jeers and threats at them. After much pleading, the Jews convinced the camp commanders to erect a fence between themselves and the German POWs. Camp B70 was located in the middle of the woods. It was surrounded by barbed wire, and there were six machine gun towers around the perimeter. The internees lived in wooden barracks and spent their daytime hours chopping wood in the forest. Their uniforms had a large red circle on the back, like a target for the guards in case someone tried to escape. The teen refugees became known as the "Camp Boys."

**Camp B70, Ripples, New Brunswick**
When the Jewish refugees arrived at Ripples, pictured in this painting on the right, it already held Nazi German prisoners of war. The Nazis had been captured by the British and sent to Canada for internment for the duration of the war.

**Forestry work**
Ripples was set in the middle of the woods. Internees spent their days cutting trees and chopping wood in the forest. The wood was used to fuel the 100 wood stoves that heated the wooden barracks.

**Targeted**
In this painting by internee Oscar Bendl, you can see the men's uniforms, denim clothing and jackets with a large red circle on the back. The Jews, who became known as the "Camp Boys," suspected that the circle was a target for the guards in case anyone tried to escape. "We thought it was very funny," Edgar Lion said. "Where would we escape to?"

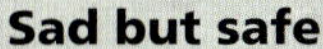

**Making socks**
The internees were put to work in a variety of ways. These Jewish men, pictured here in 1940, are making socks for the soldiers overseas. In the Sherbrooke camp, internees had the option to either make fishing nets or make socks on a sock machine that Edgar Lion described as a medieval torture apparatus.

**Sad but safe**
A young Jewish internee sits on his bed beside his cupboard that contains the personal belongings he was allowed to bring with him from Britain, including his menorah. Being interned by a country that he considered an ally would have been almost unbearable. Although the local Jewish Canadian organizations expressed their opposition to the government's decision to intern the refugees, they also felt that the interned Jews were at least safe and being fed and sheltered in Canada. They concentrated their efforts on getting more Jews out of Europe.

# Refugees Released

In 1941, the British government decided to use the Jewish men for the war effort. They could either return to Britain and join the military or obtain a sponsor and stay in Canada. Those who stayed in Canada were kept in camps for up to three years while going through the immigration system. That meant they needed a sponsor, a job and a place to stay. While they waited, some were put to war work, and the youth were allowed to continue their education. At the time, Canada did not allow Jews to immigrate, so settling the refugees was not a government priority. Finding sponsors for them fell to the Jewish community organizations.

**War work**
Many of the Jewish refugees were highly skilled and considered valuable to the allied war effort. When given the choice to stay or go back to Britain, refugee Edgar Lion (pictured here) opted to stay. He was sponsored by relatives in Montreal. He enrolled at McGill University and completed his engineering degree. While others waited to be sponsored, the Canadian government enlisted their help. These Jewish refugees at Camp N, Sherbrooke, are engaged in war work.

*"Inasmuch as ye have done it unto one of these...ye have done it unto Me"*

Something Every Warm-Hearted Canadian Should Know About the

**REFUGEE PETITION**

**WHY IS CANADA AT WAR?**

Is it not simply to preserve a place in the world for human decency? Is it not because we believe no man or race has the right to enslave or destroy another man or race? Is our unaccountable expenditure of lives, labor and wealth justifiable for any lower reason?

If the cause of humanity is worth such an effort, it is also worth the consideration of the plight of a few thousand refugees at present stranded mainly in Portugal. Putting it another way, the whole Canadian war effort is weakened unless the principles which motivate it are applied in the specific, immediate and practical issues. Fighting Hitlerism means fighting Hitler's most bestial acts. It means rescuing those whom he would kill, giving sanctuary to those lucky enough to escape from him. It means admitting some of those refugees to Canada.

All this should be obvious. But it is not. Canada, one of the richest and most sincere of the United Nations, should be first in giving refugees the right and room to live, which they were robbed of by Hitler. But she is among the last.

THE CANADIAN GOVERNMENT is presently being petitioned to offer haven to these derelicts. Because many readers of this newspaper might not otherwise have an opportunity to join in the petition, it is printed herewith. It should be clipped, signed and mailed immediately by all Canadians who believe in what they are fighting for. To refrain from signing it is to endorse the present attitude toward the refugees, an attitude little better than Hitler's.

Meanwhile it might be pointed out that at the very outside there are probably no more than 15,000 or 20,000 victims of Nazi tyranny who are in a position to come to this or any other sheltered land, and of these Canada might be expected to take in only a thousand or so. And, although the Government recently announced that a representative would be sent to Lisbon to facilitate the entry of refugees into Canada, how much Canada will actually do will undoubtedly be greatly influenced by the number of signatures secured for this petition.

Let Canada remove this moat from her eye so that she can better see the beam in Germany's. Thousands of Canadians have already written in their own blood their responsibilities to Hitler's victims. We back home can, at least, put our responsibility in ink.

WE CAN SIGN THE PETITION.

**This Appeal Is Made to You!**

**READ HOW YOU CAN HELP — BUT PLEASE ACT NOW**

*This space is contributed by the Saskatoon Branch of the CANADIAN NATIONAL COMMITTEE on Refugees and Victims of political persecution.*

DR. J. S. THOMSON, *President*

PROF. G. W. SIMPSON, *Secretary*

*Canadian National Committee on Refugees*
*220 QUEEN ST. WEST — TORONTO 2-B, CANADA*

THIS petition is to be signed by Canadian citizens of 18 years and over.
People are requested not to sign in more than one group.
Return the sheets promptly to the Committee's national headquarters or to the distributing organization

Name of Group, Church, Club., etc., and Address ..........

***Petition***

WE, the undersigned citizens of Canada, do respectfully petition His Majesty's Government and the Parliament of Canada as follows:

Realizing our responsibility in common humanity to relieve the suffering and distress of victims of Nazi terror:

We urgently entreat the Government of Canada:—

1. To offer the sanctuary of Canada to refugees from political or religious persecution without regard to race, creed or financial condition.
2. To take immediate steps to facilitate the entry into Canada of refugees (especially those stranded in Portugal) whom it is still possible to rescue.
3. To make any changes in the Immigration Act, Regulations or administration thereof necessary to admit such refugees into Canada.

***Signatures***

| NAME | ADDRESS | NAME | ADDRESS |
| --- | --- | --- | --- |
| | | | |

Signature and Address of Group Officer ..........

**Pro-refugee petition**
The Canadian government eventually agreed to release some of the refugees from Britain provided that they were sponsored by Canadians. This pro-refugee petition was published in the Saskatoon *Star Phoenix* newspaper on December 7, 1943. Canadian citizens were asked to join in the fight to increase Jewish immigration to Canada to save lives. They were also looking for Canadian sponsors for Jewish refugees, including those wrongly interned.

**Yeshiva students**
During their internment, young men were allowed to continue their education in a makeshift Yeshiva, a Jewish religious school. These students are pursuing their religious studies in Camp I, Île-aux-Noix/ Fort Lennox, south of Montreal, around 1941/42. Several later became rabbis in Canada.

## While they waited for their release, the youth were allowed to continue their education.

**Graduates**
While they waited for their release, internees were allowed to set up classes where the older educated men taught the younger boys. Some professors from McGill University in Montreal gave classes at Camp N in Sherbrooke. These Jewish refugees from Britain, many just teenagers, were interned in Camp A in Farnham, southeast of Montreal. They continued their education and are seen here in a school graduation photo in 1941.

# CHAPTER 6
# OPENING DOORS

## War Orphans Project

After the war, Canadian attitudes toward immigration softened. The Canadian Jewish Congress (CJC) saw this as an opportunity to bring over Jewish war orphans. They received approval to bring in 1,000 Jewish orphans under the age of eighteen, but, to their surprise, young orphans were hard to find. This is likely because fewer young children survived the Holocaust. More boys than girls survived because they were considered to be useful in the forced labour camps and were not murdered immediately. Of the 1,123 orphans who eventually came over, 949 were between ages fifteen and eighteen, and 70 per cent were male. The Canadian Jewish community raised most of the money for the project. The money was used for reception centres, financial assistance, food, boarding, clothing, transport, staffing, rent, hospitalization, psychiatry, social workers, recreation and education.

**Plea for sponsors**
This CJC brochure asks people to take in the war orphans that are being brought to Canada.

**Teenagers arrive**
As a result of relentless pressure from the CJC, over a thousand Jewish orphans came to Canada from 1947 to 1949. These teens have just arrived at Pier 21 in Halifax, Nova Scotia. From here, the young people dispersed and settled in thirty-eight communities across the country where each one was sponsored by a local family.

Watch the video at http://bit.ly/rcwstlouis06

**Orphans on their way**
Of the 1,123 Jewish orphans that came to Canada, 70 per cent (786) were adolescent boys, and only thirty-seven of them were under ten years old. These teen boys are en route to their new homes in 1947.

**Enjoying Canadian life**
A group of teen war orphans are pictured here at a baseball game in Winnipeg in 1948.

**Thank you**
Samuel Bronfman, president of the Canadian Jewish Congress (CJC), receives a Torah (Hebrew scripture) from two young people who were brought to Canada in 1947 as part of the Orphan Project.

## 1,123 Jewish war orphans came to Canada in 1947.

# Welcome to Canada

After the war, Canada's economy was booming. The loss of men and women to the war, combined with the economic upturn, resulted in a labour shortage. The government decided it was to Canada's advantage, not a humanitarian issue, to welcome Displaced Persons (DPs) from Europe. In 1948, the government eased their immigration restrictions and many more people became qualified to come. From 1945 to 1948, 65,000 refugees were admitted to Canada; 8,000 were Jewish. Eventually, 40,000 Holocaust survivors came to Canada seeking new lives in what they felt was a peaceful country. It took until 1978 for the Immigration Act to separate refugees from other classes of immigrants. In addition, the government's priorities for immigrants changed from race, nationality and language to those of family reunion, diversity and non-discrimination.

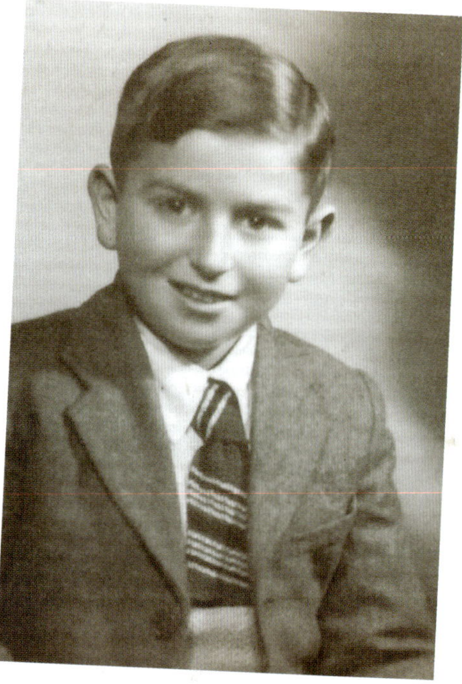

**Survivor**
Ten-year-old Mark Nusbaum, a Holocaust survivor, is pictured here in Antwerp, Belgium, just after the end of the war in 1945. He immigrated to Canada in May 1948 with his mother and stepfather.

**Source of postwar immigrants**
Canada's postwar immigrants came from many different places. This graphic indicates the ethnic origin of postwar immigrants from 1946 to 1951. Ethnic origin was determined by the father's language, except for those from the US and British Isles (includes Scotch, Welsh and Irish).

**Waiting to come to Canada**

Fifteen-year-old Regina Bulwik received this ID card while awaiting release from a Displaced Persons camp in Fulda, Germany, in 1946. A Displaced Persons camp was a temporary shelter for people whose homes and lives had been destroyed by the war in Europe.

**Refugees arrive**

Following the war, Canada had a labour shortage, and it was considered an economic advantage to welcome Displaced Persons from Europe. These Displaced Persons are arriving in Canada on the SS *Beaverbrae* in 1948.

**Refugees from Portugal**
This Jewish refugee family from Portugal has just arrived in Montreal.

**Finally here**
A group of Jewish immigrants on board the SS *General Sturgis* arrive in Halifax, Nova Scotia, on February 6, 1948. They were sponsored by the Jewish Immigrant Aid Society.

**Arriving in Halifax**
These Jewish refugees have just arrived by ship to Halifax. They are filling out the necessary immigration paperwork while Noa Heinish (far right) of the Canadian Jewish Congress looks on. The CJC took advantage of Canada's need to fill the labour shortage and convinced the government to increase their quotas of Jewish refugee immigrants.

**Help for newcomers**
Women from the Jewish Immigrant Aid Society welcome a young refugee from a Displaced Persons camp in Europe.

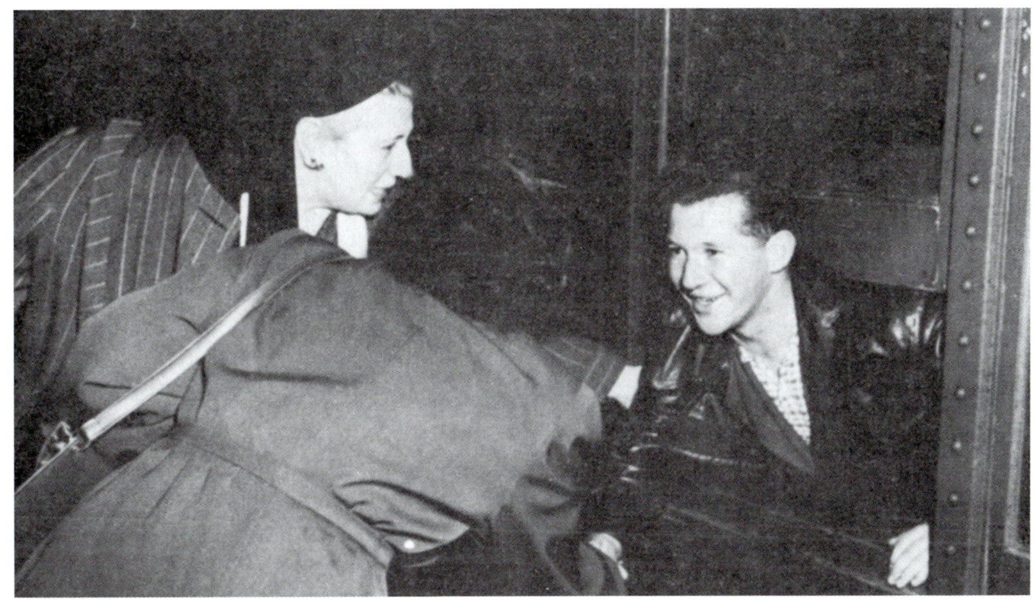

**Hard at work**
Jewish women are hard at work in a clothing industry shop in postwar Montreal. Canada gave priority to immigrants who were healthy, skilled workers. Immigration officials were not overly sympathetic to the plight of European war refugees, especially if they were Jewish.

Canada gave priority to immigrants who were healthy, skilled workers. The government increased their quotas of Jewish refugee immigrants.

# The Tailor Project

In late 1947 and early 1948, representatives of the Canadian garment industry organized what became known as the Tailor Project. It was a plan to select more than 2,200 skilled tailors from the Displaced Persons camps of Europe and give them jobs and housing in Canada. Thousands of people applied. To be accepted, they had to pass a test of sewing on either a pocket or a button hole. Those who were accepted traveled by ship to Halifax where they were put on trains for their designated destination: Montreal, Toronto or Winnipeg. In each city, the Jewish Immigrant Aid Society (JIAS) had secured work and housing for the tailors.

**Morris Dublin**
Morris Dublin was a master tailor in Poland when the war broke out. When the Germans invaded Poland in 1939, Morris Dublin escaped to the Soviet Union with his wife. They lived there throughout the war.

## 2,200 skilled tailors were part of the Tailor Project.

**Families lost**
Here, Morris and his wife, Rose Gail, are pictured with their first daughter, Devorah, who died in 1942. Morris and Gail returned to Poland at the end of the war. Sadly, they discovered that their families and homes had been wiped out by the Nazis.

Watch the video at http://bit.ly/rcwstlouis07

**Displaced Persons camp**
In 1946, the young Dublin family made their way to a Displaced Persons camp near Salzburg, Austria. Displaced Persons camps were temporary facilities established after the Second World War for Eastern European refugees.

**Safe in Canada**
Morris applied for the Tailor Project in 1948 and was accepted. He was not supposed to be eligible because he had a wife and three children by then, and regulations stipulated that only families of two children or less would be qualified. However, because he was an exceptionally skilled tailor, he was accepted. The family sailed on the SS *Samaria* and arrived in Canada in September 1948. Here he is pictured with two of his children, Anne and Max, at Sunnyside pool, Toronto.

Watch the video at http://bit.ly/rcwstlouis08

**New business**
After arriving in Canada, Morris worked for about ten years for Lloyd Brothers Custom Tailors on King Street West, Toronto. Afterward, he opened his own dry cleaning and tailoring shop, shown here. He always said, "Canada is the best country in the world."

CHAPTER 7

# ACKNOWLEDGING THE PAST

## Fighting for an Apology

On November 5, 2000, members of the Canadian clergy gathered in Ottawa to apologize to twenty-five surviving passengers of the MS *St. Louis*. One of the clergy present was Baptist minister Doug Blair, the great nephew of Frederick Blair, Director of Immigration in 1939. Doug Blair told the survivors, "I'm sorry. Will you forgive me?" In 2012, the US State Department issued an apology for turning away the passengers of the MS *St. Louis*. Those who attended called it "a low-key affair." It took another six years before the Canadian government apologized.

Jewish organizations, including the Centre for Israel and Jewish Affairs (CIJA), the Friends of Simon Wiesenthal Centre (FSWC) and B'nai Brith Canada spent years petitioning the Canadian government for a formal apology for "The *St. Louis* Affair."

**Centre for Israel and Jewish Affairs**
Shimon Fogel, pictured here, was CEO of the Centre for Israel and Jewish Affairs (CIJA) when its members were part of the lobby to convince the government to apologize for "The *St. Louis* Affair." CIJA replaced the Canadian Jewish Congress and other Canadian Jewish advocacy groups in 2004.

**B'nai Brith Canada**
This image shows the cover of a video produced by B'nai Brith Canada about the MS *St. Louis*. B'nai Brith is the oldest Jewish service organization in the world. Its mandate is to fight anti-Semitism and bigotry, as well as protect Jewish people and the State of Israel. The Canadian chapter supported the call for a government apology.

**The Friends of Simon Wiesenthal Center (FSWC)**
The Friends of Simon Wiesenthal Center, founded in 1977 by Rabbi Marvin Hier, is named for Nazi hunter and Holocaust survivor Simon Wiesenthal, pictured above with his wife, Avita. The organization is "committed to countering racism and anti-Semitism and to promoting the principles of tolerance, social justice and Canadian democratic values through advocacy and education." They are guided by the words of Simon Wiesenthal, who said, "Freedom is not a gift from Heaven. One must fight for it every day." Members of FSWC helped fight to get an apology for the MS *St. Louis* tragedy.

"Freedom is not a gift from Heaven. One must fight for it every day."

— Simon Wiesenthal, Nazi hunter and Holocaust survivor

# We Are Sorry

Prime Minister Justin Trudeau gave the overdue apology on November 7, 2018, in the House of Commons. The Prime Minister formally apologized to the passengers, their families and Jewish communities in Canada and around the world.

**Prime Minister Trudeau's apology**
These are a sample of the ten pages of the official apology that was delivered by Trudeau on November 7, 2018.

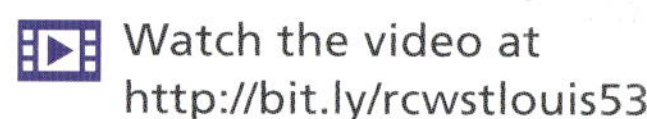
Watch the video at http://bit.ly/rcwstlouis53

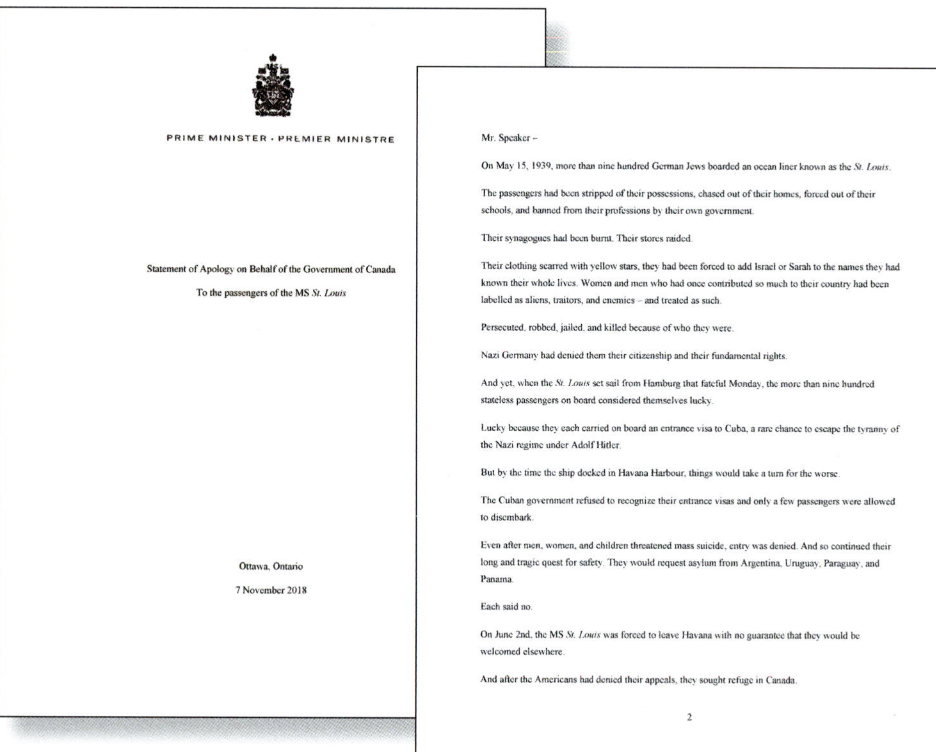

PRIME MINISTER · PREMIER MINISTRE

Statement of Apology on Behalf of the Government of Canada

To the passengers of the MS *St. Louis*

Ottawa, Ontario

7 November 2018

Mr. Speaker –

On May 15, 1939, more than nine hundred German Jews boarded an ocean liner known as the *St. Louis*.

The passengers had been stripped of their possessions, chased out of their homes, forced out of their schools, and banned from their professions by their own government.

Their synagogues had been burnt. Their stores raided.

Their clothing scarred with yellow stars, they had been forced to add Israel or Sarah to the names they had known their whole lives. Women and men who had once contributed so much to their country had been labelled as aliens, traitors, and enemies – and treated as such.

Persecuted, robbed, jailed, and killed because of who they were.

Nazi Germany had denied them their citizenship and their fundamental rights.

And yet, when the *St. Louis* set sail from Hamburg that fateful Monday, the more than nine hundred stateless passengers on board considered themselves lucky.

Lucky because they each carried on board an entrance visa to Cuba, a rare chance to escape the tyranny of the Nazi regime under Adolf Hitler.

But by the time the ship docked in Havana Harbour, things would take a turn for the worse.

The Cuban government refused to recognize their entrance visas and only a few passengers were allowed to disembark.

Even after men, women, and children threatened mass suicide, entry was denied. And so continued their long and tragic quest for safety. They would request asylum from Argentina, Uruguay, Paraguay, and Panama.

Each said no.

On June 2nd, the MS *St. Louis* was forced to leave Havana with no guarantee that they would be welcomed elsewhere.

And after the Americans had denied their appeals, they sought refuge in Canada.

2

## Quotes from the pages of the apology

"The Government of Canada was indifferent to the suffering of Jews long before the *St. Louis* ever set sail for Halifax, and sadly, long after it had returned to Europe … To the government of the day, Jews were among the least desirable immigrants; their presence on our soil had to be limited. The government imposed strict quotas and an ever-growing list of requirements designed to deter Jewish immigration."

"Bitter resentment towards Jews was enshrined in our policies — the same policies immigration officials would later use to justify their callous response to the *St. Louis* and its passengers."

"Today, I rise in this House to issue a long overdue apology to the Jewish refugees Canada turned away. We apologize to the 907 German Jews aboard the MS *St. Louis*, as well as their families. We also apologize to others who paid the price of our inaction, whom we doomed to the ultimate horror of the death camps. We used our laws to mask our anti-Semitism, our antipathy and our resentment. We are sorry for the callousness of Canada's response. And we are sorry for not apologizing sooner. We apologize to the mothers and fathers whose children we did not save, to the daughters and sons whose parents we did not help — To the imprisoned Jewish refugees who were forced to relive their trauma next to their tormentors …"

"To harbour such hatred and indifference towards the refugees was to share in the moral responsibility for their deaths. And while decades have passed since we turned our backs on Jewish refugees, time has by no means absolved Canada of its guilt or lessened the weight of its shame."

"And finally, we apologize to the members of Canada's Jewish community whose voices were ignored, whose calls went unanswered. We were quick to forget the many ways in which they had helped build this country since its inception. Quick to forget that they were our friends and neighbours. That they had educated our youth, cared for our sick, and clothed our poor. Instead, we let anti-Semitism take hold in our communities and become our official policy."

"Mr. Speaker — it is my sincere hope that by issuing this long overdue apology, we can shine a light on this painful chapter of our history and ensure that its lessons are never forgotten."

**Apology ceremony**
Descendants of the Spitz family, who were MS *St. Louis* survivors, pose for a family photo at the official apology in Ottawa in 2018.

**Canada apologizes**
Prime Minister Justin Trudeau delivers the MS *St. Louis* apology in the House of Commons on November 7, 2018.

**Prime Minister Trudeau meets with a survivor**
Trudeau is pictured here in conversation with Ana Maria Gordon (nee Karman) in Toronto. Ana Maria was four years old when she sailed on the MS *St. Louis* with her parents. Trudeau's Twitter says, "Ana Maria Gordon is the only surviving passenger of the MS *St. Louis* living in Canada. I met with her today ahead of our government's apology in the House of Commons. Thank you, Ana Maria, for coming here, thank you for your testimony, and thank you for being part of this moment."

Ana Maria attended the apology in Ottawa with her children and grandchildren. She stated, "This apology is meaningful for me. I feel blessed to call Canada my home — this great country where we live free regardless of race, religion or colour."

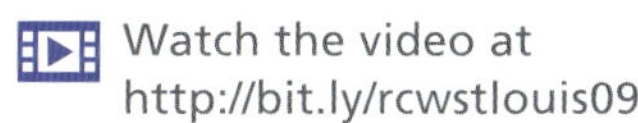


Watch the video at http://bit.ly/rcwstlouis09

**A happy occasion**
Many members of Canada's Jewish community, like these people, attended the apology ceremony in Ottawa. Reaction to the apology was positive. Avi Benlolo, president and CEO of the Friends of Simon Wiesenthal Center, stated, "This is an important acknowledgement by the prime minister. As anti-Semitism has once more risen in Canada, this provides an additional opportunity for the government to address contemporary issues. By recognizing such wrongs committed in the past, we can move toward creating a Canada that is truly dedicated to standing up for tolerance, acceptance and diversity."

"By recognizing such wrongs committed in the past, we can move toward creating a Canada that is truly dedicated to standing up for tolerance, acceptance and diversity."

# Overcoming Anti-Semitism in Canada

In the years since the war, Jews have thrived in Canada, overcoming anti-Semitism. Jews have succeeded in a wide variety of fields including medicine, law, business, construction, education and entertainment. Jews have contributed to every aspect of Canadian life. Holocaust survivors, who came to Canada with nothing, have raised families, started businesses, contributed to medical research and lead successful lives.

As the community looks to the future, it continues to build on the past. When Canada opened its doors to immigrants, it ushered in an era of progress, not only for Jews but for all immigrants from other cultures that have come here to seek freedom, economic opportunity and peace.

In his apology, the Prime Minister warned of an "alarming rate" of discrimination and violence against Jewish people today. According to the most recent figures, 17 per cent of all hate crimes in Canada target Jewish people; far higher per capita than any other group. "We must guard our communities and institutions against the kinds of evils that took hold in the hearts of so many, more than seventy years ago, for they did not end with the war," Mr. Trudeau said. "More than seventy years ago, Canada turned its back on you, but today, Canadians pledge, now and forever, never again." May that pledge extend to people from anywhere who want to live in peace and freedom in a country that respects their culture.

**David Croll**
In 1935, Russian immigrant David Croll became the first Jewish cabinet member in Ontario. He served as a lieutenant-colonel in the Second World War and in 1945, was elected as the only Toronto federal Liberal. Despite being re-elected two more times, neither Prime Ministers Mackenzie King nor Louis St. Laurent would put him in cabinet because he was Jewish. In 1955, Croll became the country's first Jewish senator and served until his death in 1991.

**New government policy of multiculturalism**

In the 1970s, Prime Minister Pierre Elliott Trudeau (father of Justin Trudeau), pictured here, made multiculturalism a major platform of his government. The new policy affected Canadian attitudes and improved the lives of Jews and other minorities. Pierre Trudeau appointed many Jews to his cabinet, the judiciary and the civil service. Herb Gray became the first Jewish federal cabinet minister in 1969 and later served as deputy prime minister. David Lewis was the first Jew to lead a national political party, the New Democratic Party (NDP). Israel Asper was elected leader of the Manitoba Liberal Party in 1970, and David Barrett of British Columbia became the first Jewish premier in 1972.

**What became of the war orphans?**

In his apology, Prime Minister Justin Trudeau declared, "Jewish Canadians have made immense contributions to our country. As do all the immigrants who have chosen and continue to choose Canada." Many of the war orphans who arrived postwar have had remarkably successful lives. For example, Sam Ganz founded the multimillion-dollar Ganz Toy Company that makes, among other things, the Webkinz brand of stuffed animals pictured left. Other successful individuals include Leslie Dan who created the pharmaceutical giant Novopharm and became a billionaire philanthropist and recipient of the Order of Canada. Joseph Rothbart spent fifty-one years as the executive director of Montreal's Mount Sinai Hospital. Filmmaker Jack Kuper directed acclaimed independent movies, and John Freund penned numerous memoirs. John Hirsch was co-artistic director at the Stratford Festival (1967–1969), head of television drama for the CBC (1974–1978) and artistic director at the Stratford Festival (1981–1985).

**Rosalie Abella, Supreme Court Judge**

Rosalie Silberman Abella was born in a displaced persons camp in Stuttgart, Germany in 1946. She and her family came to Canada in 1950 as refugees after the Second World War. She was a judge for 30 years before becoming the first Jewish woman appointed to the Canadian Supreme Court in 2004. Northwestern Pritzker School of Law's Center for International Human Rights named her the Global Jurist of the Year in 2016 for her lifelong commitment to human rights and international criminal justice.

**Leonard Cohen, Musician, Poet**
Born in Westmount, Quebec, Leonard Cohen was a Canadian singer, songwriter, poet and novelist. He was an international success and highly respected in Canada. He was a member of the Canadian Music Hall of Fame, the Canadian Songwriters Hall of Fame and the Rock and Roll Hall of Fame. Leonard Cohen died in November 2016, at the age of 82.

**Drake, Musician**
Aubrey "Drake" Graham was born in 1986 in Toronto, Ontario. His father is an African-American musician, and his mother is a Jewish-Canadian educator. As a child, Drake attended a Jewish day school, and formally celebrated a Bar Mitzvah. Drake's first success came when he was fifteen, playing the character "Jimmy Brooks" on the popular series, *Degrassi: the Next Generation.* In 2006, Drake launched his music career. He has won many awards including five Junos, three Grammys and two MTV Video Music awards. In September 2013, Drake was named a global ambassador for the National Basketball Association's Toronto Raptors. He helped to rebrand the team, which involved the new "We the North" marketing campaign, as well as a new logo and uniform design.

**Linda Frum, Senator**
Canadian Senator Linda Frum was born in Toronto, Ontario in 1963. She became a columnist with the *National Post*, a contributing editor to *Maclean's* magazine and a Gemini-Award winning documentarian. Frum was appointed to the Senate of Canada in 2009. She is a staunch advocate for human rights and has received many awards for her principles and leadership. Frum successfully introduced the Canadian Jewish Heritage Month Act (Bill S-232) to Parliament to educate future generations about the role of Jewish Canadians in shaping Canada's social, economic, political and cultural fabric.

**Naomi Klein, Author, Social Activist, Filmmaker**
Naomi Klein was born in Montreal, Quebec in 1970 to a Jewish family of peace activists. Klein's books and films deal with social issues. Her 2014 book, *This Changes Everything: Capitalism vs. the Climate*, was a New York Times best seller and won the Hilary Weston Writers' Trust Prize for Nonfiction. Two years later, she won the Sydney Peace Prize for her activism on climate justice. In 2018, she began a three-year appointment as the Gloria Steinem Chair in Media, Culture, and Feminist Studies at Rutgers University, New York.

**Eugene Levy, Co-creator of *Schitt's Creek***
Eugene Levy was born in 1946 in Hamilton, Ontario. His father's parents were Bulgarian Sephardi Jews and his mother's parents were Polish Ashkenazi Jews. Levy is an award-winning Canadian actor, comedian, producer, director and writer. In 2013, Levy formed *Not a Real Company Productions* with his son Daniel Levy and others. Together they produced the award-winning comedy television series, *Schitt's Creek*. In 2016, *Schitt's Creek* swept the Canadian Screen Awards, winning nine of a possible ten categories. In 2020, the show won 9 Emmys including Best Actor for Eugene Levy. Levy is a Member of the Order of Canada and a recipient of The Governor General's Performing Arts Award.

**Mordecai Richler, Author**
Mordecai Richler, pictured here on this mural in Montreal, was born in 1931 to an orthodox Jewish family in the St. Urbain Street neighbourhood of Montreal. In dozens of novels, screenplays and works of non-fiction, Richler wrote about growing up in the tight-knit, mostly poor and largely immigrant world of his youth. Richler's best known works are *The Apprenticeship of Duddy Kravitz* (1959) and *Barney's Version* (1997). In 1975, Richler published a novel for children, *Jacob Two-Two Meets the Hooded Fang*. It won the first Ruth Schwartz Children's Book Award in 1976. Richler was one of the most respected literary figures in Canada when he died in 2001.

**Bobbie Rosenfeld, Athlete**
Fanny "Bobbie" Rosenfeld was born in 1904 in Ukraine and came to Canada with her parents when she was less than a month old. As a young girl she excelled in track and field, ice hockey, tennis, basketball and softball. At the 1928 Summer Olympics in Amsterdam, pictured here second from the left, she won both gold and silver medals in track. Later she became a sportswriter with *The Globe and Mail*. She was inducted into the Canadian Sports Hall of Fame and was widely admired for her decency, honesty and sense of fair play.

**William Shatner, Actor**
William Shatner was born in Montreal, Quebec in 1931 to Jewish parents. Shatner began acting at eight years old as a member of the Montreal Children's Theatre. In 1954, he performed at the Stratford Shakespeare Festival and then went to Broadway, New York two years later. His big break came in 1966 when Gene Roddenberry cast him in the role of Captain James T. Kirk in the famous TV show, *Star Trek*. He also starred in some of the *Star Trek* films.

# Remembering the MS *St. Louis*

***The Wheel of Conscience***
On January 20, 2011, this memorial sculpture commemorating the *St. Louis* refugees was unveiled at the Canadian Museum of Immigration at Pier 21 in Halifax. Called *The Wheel of Conscience*, the statue is the work of American architect Daniel Libeskind and graphic designer David Berman. It is a steel sculpture comprised of four gears. The first and smallest gear, labeled *hatred*, turns increasingly larger gears that are labeled *racism*, *xenophobia* and *anti-Semitism*. The names of all the passengers who were on the ship are etched on the back of the sculpture.

A memorial to the MS *St. Louis* refugees was unveiled at Pier 21, Halifax.

**Celebrating the Canadian Jewish experience**
As part of Canada 150 in 2017, a group of Jewish activists led by Tova Lynch put together an extensive exhibit called *Canadian Jewish Experience*. The exhibit traveled across the country and internationally to raise awareness about Jews in Canada.

**Jewish Heritage Month**
On May 30, 2017, an Act of Parliament established May as Jewish Heritage Month throughout Canada. Tova Lynch, Chair of *Canadian Jewish Experience* in 2017, is pictured in the centre in a striped dress.

**Looking back**
This traveling exhibit on the MS *St. Louis* was organized by the Maritime Museum of the Atlantic, Halifax, to educate visitors about Canada's denial of entry to Jewish refugees.

## In 2017, May was established as Jewish Heritage Month throughout Canada.

# Timeline

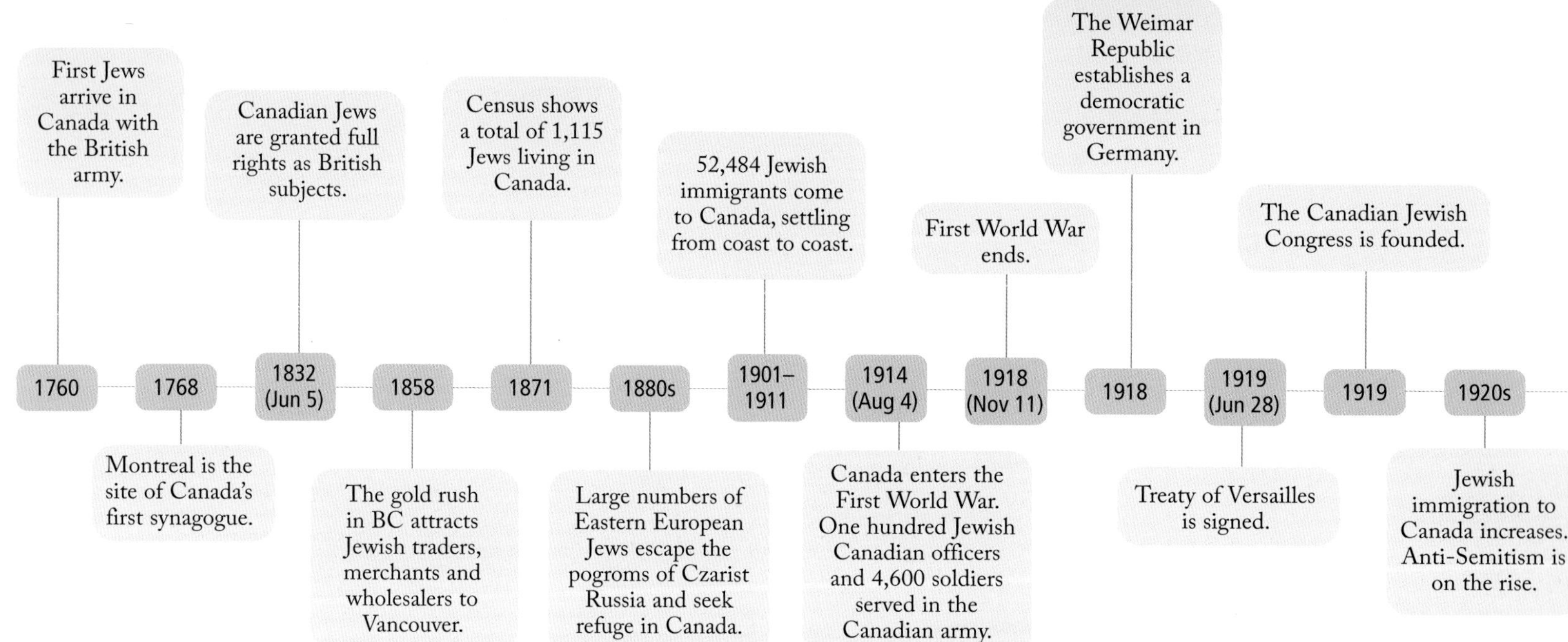


1939
Kindertransport arrives in England with 10,000 German and Austrian Jewish children.

1939 (May 15)
The MS *St. Louis* sails from Hamburg, Germany for Cuba.

1939 (May 27)
The *St. Louis* arrives in Havana harbour.

1939 (Jun 2)
Cuban President Bru orders the ship to leave Cuban waters. The *St. Louis* heads to Miami, then Canada and then back to Europe.

1939 (Jun 17)
The *St. Louis* docks in Antwerp, Belgium.

1939 (Sep 1)
The Second World War begins.

1939 (Sep 10)
Canada declares war.

1940
England sends German and Austrian Jews to Canada where they are interned in prisoner of war camps as enemy aliens.

1941–1945
The Holocaust in which six million Jews were murdered in Europe.

1941 (Dec 7)
The Japanese bomb the US Naval base at Pearl Harbor, Hawaii. The US enters the Second World War.

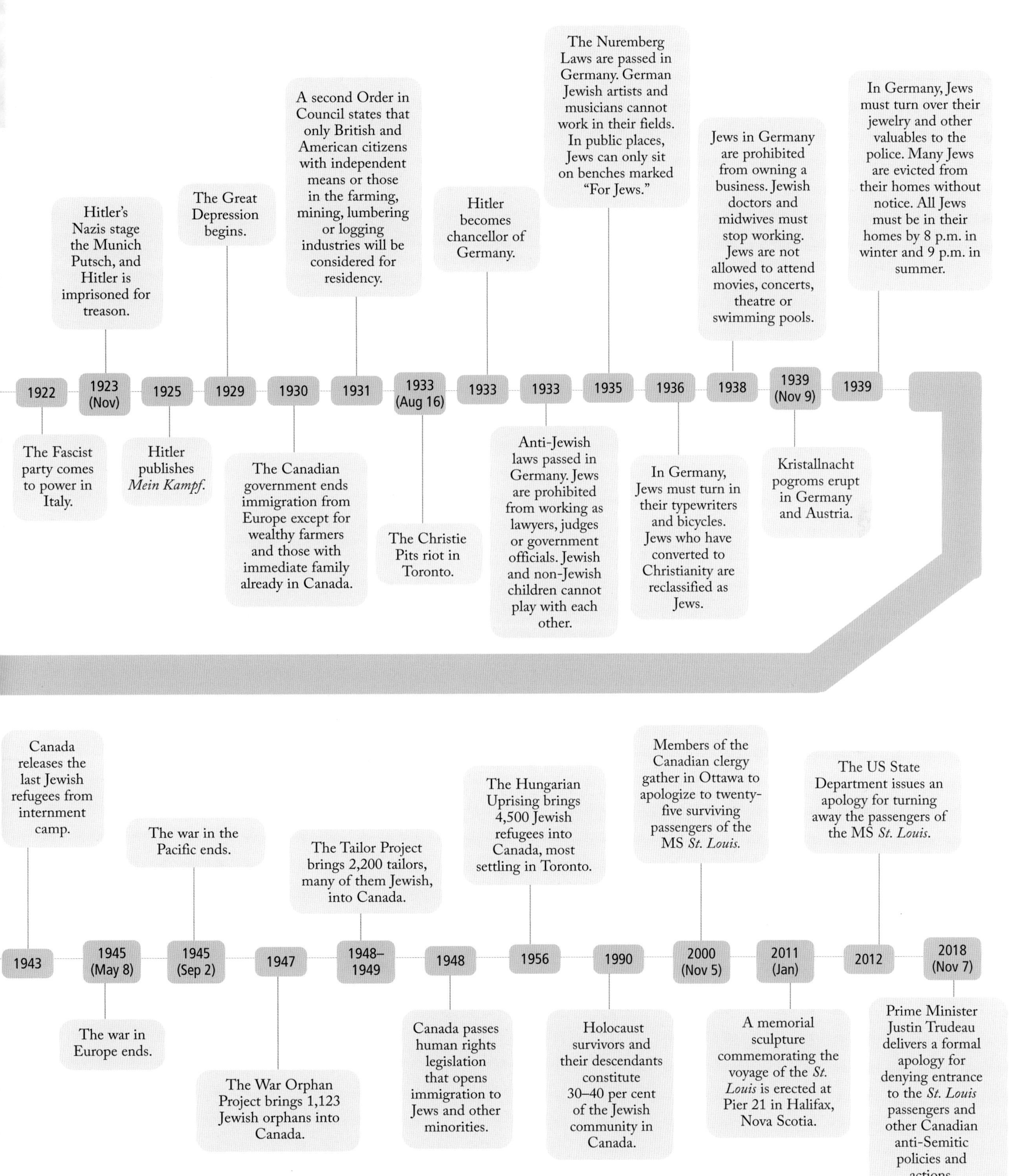
1922
The Fascist party comes to power in Italy.
1923 (Nov)
Hitler's Nazis stage the Munich Putsch, and Hitler is imprisoned for treason.
1925
Hitler publishes *Mein Kampf*.
1929
The Great Depression begins.
1930
The Canadian government ends immigration from Europe except for wealthy farmers and those with immediate family already in Canada.
1931
A second Order in Council states that only British and American citizens with independent means or those in the farming, mining, lumbering or logging industries will be considered for residency.
1933 (Aug 16)
The Christie Pits riot in Toronto.
1933
Hitler becomes chancellor of Germany.
1933
Anti-Jewish laws passed in Germany. Jews are prohibited from working as lawyers, judges or government officials. Jewish and non-Jewish children cannot play with each other.
1935
The Nuremberg Laws are passed in Germany. German Jewish artists and musicians cannot work in their fields. In public places, Jews can only sit on benches marked "For Jews."
1936
In Germany, Jews must turn in their typewriters and bicycles. Jews who have converted to Christianity are reclassified as Jews.
1938
Jews in Germany are prohibited from owning a business. Jewish doctors and midwives must stop working. Jews are not allowed to attend movies, concerts, theatre or swimming pools.
1939 (Nov 9)
Kristallnacht pogroms erupt in Germany and Austria.
1939
In Germany, Jews must turn over their jewelry and other valuables to the police. Many Jews are evicted from their homes without notice. All Jews must be in their homes by 8 p.m. in winter and 9 p.m. in summer.
1943
Canada releases the last Jewish refugees from internment camp.
1945 (May 8)
The war in Europe ends.
1945 (Sep 2)
The war in the Pacific ends.
1947
The War Orphan Project brings 1,123 Jewish orphans into Canada.
1948–1949
The Tailor Project brings 2,200 tailors, many of them Jewish, into Canada.
1948
Canada passes human rights legislation that opens immigration to Jews and other minorities.
1956
The Hungarian Uprising brings 4,500 Jewish refugees into Canada, most settling in Toronto.
1990
Holocaust survivors and their descendants constitute 30–40 per cent of the Jewish community in Canada.
2000 (Nov 5)
Members of the Canadian clergy gather in Ottawa to apologize to twenty-five surviving passengers of the MS *St. Louis*.
2011 (Jan)
A memorial sculpture commemorating the voyage of the *St. Louis* is erected at Pier 21 in Halifax, Nova Scotia.
2012
The US State Department issues an apology for turning away the passengers of the MS *St. Louis*.
2018 (Nov 7)
Prime Minister Justin Trudeau delivers a formal apology for denying entrance to the *St. Louis* passengers and other Canadian anti-Semitic policies and actions.

# Glossary

**Anti-Semitism**: Hatred of, or discrimination against, individuals because of their Jewish heritage.

**Aryan**: The term Nazis used to describe people they believed were of pure German blood. The ideal Aryan was white with blond hair and blue eyes.

**Ashkenazi**: Eastern European Jews.

**B'nai Brith**: A Jewish service organization committed to the security and continuity of the Jewish people and dedicated to combatting anti-Semitism, racism and bigotry.

**Civil rights**: The basic privileges that come with being a member of society in a certain country. Rights such as the right to vote, have an education and receive justice in the courts are civil rights.

**Concentration camps**: A term that refers to the crowding together of people in a confined space by authorities. They were established by the Nazis before and during the Second World War for the imprisonment and persecution of Jews, other minorities and political prisoners.

**Culture**: The customs, traditions and values of an ethnic group, a country or its people.

**Diaspora**: The movement or spread of people away from their homeland.

**Discrimination**: Unjust actions that are caused by a particular mindset or prejudice; a means of treating people negatively because of their group identity. Discrimination may be based on age, ancestry, gender, language, race, religion, political beliefs, sexual orientation, family status, physical or mental disability, appearance or economic status. Acts of discrimination hurt, humiliate and isolate the victim.

**Displaced Persons**: People driven from their homeland by circumstances such as war, persecution or famine.

**Enemy Alien**: A person of foreign descent living in a country that is at war with his country of ancestry. In Canada, it was applied regardless of birthplace or citizenship and required no proof of crimes against Canada.

**Fascism**: A political movement that believes in absolute control of a nation under a single authority, or dictator. It does not allow for any opposition and will use violence to crush it. The Nazis were a Fascist party. Amongst other things, Fascism promotes the hatred of Jews, the belief in a superior national race and total service to the nation by all. A governmental system led by a dictator having complete power, forcibly suppressing opposition and criticism, emphasizing an aggressive nationalism and often promoting racism. A follower is called a fascist.

**Fifth column**: A group within a country at war who are secretly working for the enemy. Fear of a fifth column has led governments who are at war to label some of their citizens as Enemy Aliens, and even detain them in internment camps.

**Fuehrer**: The German word meaning "leader" that was applied to Hitler.

**Gentile**: A person who is not Jewish; often refers to a Christian.

**Ghetto**: An area of a city in which Jews were forced to live in cramped, dangerous conditions. The first ghetto was in Venice, Italy, in 1516. During the Second World War, the Nazis set up Jewish ghettos in occupied cities and towns.

**Great Depression**: A time between 1930 and 1939 when Canada experienced a long-term downturn in economic activity.

**Hebrew**: The ancient language of the Jewish people and the language spoken in Israel today.

**The Holocaust**: The mass murder of the Jews and other minorities by the Nazis from 1941–45.

**Immigrant**: A person who moves to another country, usually as a permanent resident.

**Israel**: The modern Jewish state in the Middle East, established in 1948. The "Land of Israel" is also the traditional name for the ancient Hebrew nation (930–721 BCE).

**Internment**: The confinement of people labelled enemies of the state during wartime. Canada interned thousands of individuals of Japanese and European descent, including Italians, Germans and Jews.

**Internment camp**: The place where thousands of individuals whom Canada labelled enemy aliens were held.

**Jew**: A member of an ethnic and religious group who follows Judaism.

**Kristallnacht**: The German government's organized violence against Jews on November 9–10, 1938. The name comes from the German words meaning "Night of Broken Glass."

**Kindertransport**: The evacuation of 10,000 children from Germany and Austria to England between 1938 and 1940.

***Mein Kampf***: A book by Hitler published in 1925 describing his personal struggles and outlining his plans for the Nazi Party.

**Middle Ages**: The period of European history between the 5th and 15th centuries.

**Nazi**: A member of the National Socialist German Workers' Party, which controlled Germany from 1933 to 1945 under Adolf Hitler. The Nazi Party practiced a one-party government that believed in territorial expansion, anti-Semitism and Aryan supremacy.

**Nuremberg Laws**: Laws enacted by the Nazis in 1935 that took away citizenship and basic civil rights from German Jews and prohibited them from marrying or having sexual relations with persons of "German or related blood."

**Palestine**: Traditionally, the area of the Middle East that once included what is now Israel and Jordan. Today it is made up of the West Bank and Gaza.

**Pale of Settlement**: The only part of the Russian Empire where Jews were allowed to live from 1791 to 1917.

**Pogrom**: An organized attack on a minority group, especially Jews.

**Prejudice**: An attitude, usually negative, directed toward a person or group of people based on wrong or distorted information. Prejudiced thinking may result in acts of discrimination.

**Propaganda**: The spread of specific information, ideas or images (such as anti-Jewish pictures or war posters) to influence and control public opinion or actions.

**Racism**: A belief that one race is superior to another. People are not treated as equals because of their cultural or ethnic differences. Racism may be systemic (part of institutions, governments, organizations and programs) or part of the attitudes and behaviour of individuals.

**Refugee**: A person who flees a country to escape a war or political persecution.

**Reparations**: Financial compensation paid by a defeated country to another country, or to an individual, for loss suffered as a result of war. Making amends for a wrong one has done, by paying money to, or otherwise helping, the wronged side. Refers to the money that Germany was required to pay the allies after the First and Second World Wars.

**Revolution**: The overthrow of a government by force.

**Sephardic**: Jews who descended from Spanish or Portuguese Jews.

**Synagogue**: A building used for Jewish worship, study and celebrations.

**Swastika**: The official emblem of the Nazi party and the Third Reich, and a symbol of fascism.

**Third Reich**: The German government from 1933 to 1945.

**Torah**: The Jewish sacred writings. They are the first five books of the Hebrew Bible generally attributed to Moses.

**Treaty of Versailles**: The document created at the end of the First World War that held Germany responsible for starting the war and outlined the conditions of peace. It was signed on June 28, 1919, at the Paris Peace Conference in France.

**Visa**: A document that allows a person to legally enter a country.

**Yiddish**: The language of Eastern European Jews. It is based on Hebrew and German, with words from other languages, such as Polish and Russian.

**Zionism**: The movement for a Jewish nation in the area that is now Israel. Modern Zionism was established in 1897 by Theodor Hertzl, a Jewish journalist in Austria who believed the Jewish people needed a homeland.

# For Further Reading

**Books**

Arato, Rona. *The Last Train, a Holocaust Story*. Toronto, Owlkids Books, 2013.

*The Ship to Nowhere*. Toronto, Second Story Press, 2016.

Berne, Emma Carlson. *Escaping the Nazis on the Kindertransport*. Encounter: Narrative Nonfiction Stories, 2017.

Correa, Lucas. *The German Girl*. New York, Atria Books, 2016.

Drucker, Olga Levy. *Kindertransport*. New York, Henry Holt & Company, 1992.

Golabek, Mona. *The Children of Willesden Lane: A True Story of Hope and Survival During World War II (Young Readers Edition)*. Lebanon, IN, Hachette Book Group, 2017.

Hodge, Deborah. *Rescuing the Children: The Story of the Kindertransport*. New York, Penguin Random House, 2012.

Hopkinson, Deborah. *We Had to Be Brave*: *Escaping the Nazis on the Kindertransport*. Scholastic Focus, 2020.

Kacer, Kathy. *To Hope and Back*. Toronto, Second Story Press, 2011.

Lawler, Alison. *The Saddest Ship Afloat*. Halifax: Nimbus Publishing, 2016.

Levitt, Cyril and William Shaffir. *The Riot at Christie Pits*. University of Toronto Press, Toronto, 2018.

Matas, Carol. *Dear Canada: Turned Away. The World War II Diary of Devorah Bernstein, Winnipeg, Manitoba, 1941*. Toronto, Scholastic Canada, 2005.

*Pieces of the Past*. Toronto, Scholastic Canada, 2013.

*The Holocaust Diary of Rose Rabinowitz, Winnipeg, Manitoba, 1948*. Toronto, Scholastic Canada, 2013.

Renaud, Anne. *Pier 21: Stories from Near and Far*. Whitecap Books Ltd., 2015.

**Videos**

*When Canada Said No: the Abandoned Jews of the St. Louis*. B'nai Brith Canada.

*The Journey, the Embrace*. Watchmen for the Nations.

# Visual Credits

Every effort has been made to locate the original copyright owners. If the reader has any additional information on the original copyright owners, we would be happy to include it in any revised editions.

American Joint Distribution Committee Archives, New York: page 49 (left, #NY_08763)

Ana Maria Gruner Collection: page 39 (all), 50 (left)

Arato Collection: page 9 (top left)

Barrington Walker, ed. *The History of Immigration and Racism in Canada* (Canadian Scholars, 2008) and City of Toronto Archives: page 15 (bottom right), 16 (top) and Esther Walerstein Grant Collection: page 15 (top right)

B'nai Brith: page 71 (left)

Canadian Jewish Congress CC National Archives: page 31 (right), 53 (top), 63 (top, middle), 66 (bottom), 67 (bottom) and Canadian Museum of Civilization: page 53 (bottom)

Cyril H. Levitt and William Shaffir, *The Riot at Christie Pitts* (Lester and Orpen Dennys, 1987): page 29 (middle), 30 (all), 31 (top left); Levitt, Shaffi and *Toronto Daily Star,* 13 April, 1933: page 28 (left); Levitt, Shaffi and *Toronto Daily Star*, 24 April, 1933: page 24 (top right)

Dr. Mark Nusbaum: page 64 (right)

Dublin Family Collection: page 68 (all), 69 (all)

Erna Paris, *Jews, An Account of their Experience in Canada* (Macmillan, 1980) and City of Toronto Archives: page 15 (top left, James Collection)

Faith in Canada 150: page 70

Franca Iacovetta, Roberto Perin and Angelo Principe, *Enemies Within: Italian and Other Internees in Canada and Abroad* (University of Toronto Press, 2000): page 60 (left), 61 (top)

George Petroff Family Collection: page 11 (bottom right)

Gerald J. J. Tulchinsky, *Branching Out: The Transformation of the Canadian Jewish Community* (Stoddart Pub, 1998): page 62 (bottom)

Harold Troper and Irving Abella, *None is Too Many: Canada and the Jews of Europe, 1933–1948* (University of Toronto Press, 1982): page 63 (bottom); Troper, Abella and Archives of Canada: page 47 (top left); Troper, Abella and *Saskatoon StarPhoenix*: page 60 (right); Troper, Abella and Joint

Distribution Committee: page 35 (top right); Troper, Abella and Canadian Pacific: page 65 (bottom); Troper, Abella and Jewish Congress Archives: page 66 (top left)

Harry Gutkin, *Journey into Our Heritage* (Dennys: 1980) and Ontario Jewish Archives: page 14 (bottom, 6718), 29 (bottom, 6161); Gutkin and Canadian Jewish Congress CC National Archives: page 34 (right); Gutkin and City of Toronto Archives: page 16 (bottom left, SC231-2206)

Hirsz Abramowicz and Dina Abramowicz, Jeffrey Shandler, eds., *Profiles of a Lost World: Memoirs of East European Jewish Life before World War Two* (Detroit: Wayne State University Press, 1999): page 8–9 (centre)

Holocaust Life Stories: page 57 (top)

Holy Land Marketplace: page 7 (second right from bottom)

Ian Kershaw, *Hitler, 1936–45 Nemesis, Volume 2* (W.W. Norton & Company: 2001): page 22 (right, bottom left, bottom right), 25 (top left, top right)

Irving Abella, *A Coat of Many Colours* (Key Porter Books, 1990): page 31 (bottom); Abella and Canadian Jewish Congress CC National Archives: page 12 (right), 29 (top), 34 (left), 35 (left, bottom right), 76; Abella and Jewish Historical Society: page 10, 52 (bottom right); Abella and BC Archives and Records Service: page 12 (bottom left); Abella and Library and Archives Canada: page 13 (bottom right, C-27450)

Japanese Canadian National Museum: page 54 (left, 1994-81-3), page 55 (bottom, 1994-69-4-16)

Jean-Francois Nadeau, *The Canadian Fuhrer: The Life of Adrien Arcand* (Toronto: James Lorimer & Company Ltd., Publishers, 2011): page 28 (bottom right)

Jewish Public Library Archives: page 59 (middle, bottom), 66 (right, 84-149), 67 (top)

Jim Lynch: page 80 (bottom)

Jews of Toronto: Dorothy Dworkin Collection: page 16 (bottom right)

Keith Minchin: page 54 (bottom), 55 (top), 57 (middle), 58 (right), 59 (top)

Laurence Rees, *Hitler's Charisma: Leading Millions into the Abyss* (Penguin Random House, 2014): page 20 (left), 24 (bottom right)

Lawrie Cate: page 7 (top left)

*Le Canard* (Montreal), Oct. 1906: page 18 (bottom)

Library and Archives Canada: page 19 (right, PA-000253-V2), 33 (top, PA-801968), 52 (left, MIKAN no. 4233813), 57 (bottom right, PA-176666), 79 (bottom left, PA-151007)

Main Street, Glace Bay, 1912. 77-90-225. Beaton Institute, Cape Breton University: page 17 (bottom)

Michael Brown, *Jew or Juif? Jews, French Canadians, and Anglo-Canadians, 1759–1914* (Jewish Publication Society, 1987) and McCord Museum, McGill University, Notman Collection: page 14 (top left); Brown and Jewish Public Library: page 13 (bottom left), 14 (right)

Michael O'Hagan: page 56

Miller Family Collection: page 74 (top)

Morris Roitman Family Collection: page 11 (top)

PMO, Government of Canada: page 72 (all), 73, 74 (bottom), 75 (all)

Rona Arato: page 7 (top right)

Rose Reisman, *Rose Reisman's Light Vegetarian Cooking* (Robert Rose Inc.: 1998): page 7 (bottom left, photo by Mark T. Shapiro)

Russ Gourluck, *The Mosaic Village: A History of Winnipeg's North End* (Great Plains Publications: 2010): page 13 (top right)

Saint John Jewish Historical Society Inc.: page 17 (top left and top right)

Senator Frum: page 78 (bottom left)

Shutterstock: page 78 (middle right, bottom right), 79 (top left)

Simon Weisenthal Center: page 71 (right)

Spitz Family Collection: page 40 (all), 41 (all), 44 (left), 51 (top left)

Studio Daniel Libeskind: page 80 (left)

Temple Lodge, No. 33: page 12 (top left)

The Canadian Jewish Experience: page 81 (all)

*The Daily Herald (*Calgary): page 32

*Toronto Saturday Night*, Dec. 1904: page 18 (right)

United States Holocaust Memorial Museum: page 23 (right), 23 (left, courtesy of Deutsches Historisches Museum GmbH), 24 (left, courtesy of Joseph Shadur), 26 (left), 26 (top right, courtesy of Anna Meyer), 26 (bottom right, courtesy of Instytut Pamieci Narodowej), 27 (bottom, courtesy of Ruth Wasserman Segal), 27 (top left, courtesy of Greta Meier), 33 (middle and bottom, courtesy of Magda Herzog Muller), 36 (top right, courtesy of Helba Loevinsohn Roubicek), 37 (top left, courtesy of Julie Klein, photo by Max Reid), 37 (right, courtesy of Fred Vendig), 37 (bottom left, courtesy of Herbert and Vera Karliner), 38 (top, courtesy of Gerri Felder, photo by Max Reid), 38 (right, courtesy of Herbert and Vera Karliner), 42 (bottom, courtesy of Fred Buff), 42 (top, courtesy of Herbert and Vera Karliner), 43 (right, courtesy of Don Altman), 43 (left, courtesy of Fred Vendig), 44 (right, courtesy of Julie Klein), 45 (middle right, bottom right, courtesy of Liesl Joseph Loeb), 45 (top, courtesy of National Archives and Records Administration, College Park), 46 (art by Sol Levenson), 47 (top right, courtesy of Betty Troper Yaeger), 47 (bottom, courtesy of Henry Gallant), 48 (left, courtesy of Fred Buff), 49 (right, courtesy of Julie Klein), 50 (bottom right, 720352), 62 (left)

Vancouver Holocaust Education Centre Archives: page 58 (left, Gunter Bardeleben Collection), 61 (bottom, Gunter Bardeleben Collection), 65 (top, Regina Feldman Collection)

Vicki Matthews: page 78 (top left)

War Museum of Canada: page 19 (top, 19820376-004)

YIVO Institute for Jewish Research Archives: page 9 (right), 25 (bottom left)

# Index